RECOVERY NOW

RECOVERY NOW

A Basic Text for Today

HAZELDEN®

Hazelden
Center City, Minnesota 55012
hazelden.org

© 2013 by Hazelden Foundation
All rights reserved. Published 2013.
Printed in the United States of America

No part of this publication, either print or electronic, may be reproduced in any form or by any means without the express written permission of the publisher. Failure to comply with these terms may expose you to legal action and damages for copyright infringement.

ISBN: 978-1-61649-507-7

Editor's note
The names, details, and circumstances may have been changed to protect the privacy of those mentioned in this publication. In some cases, composites have been created.

This publication is not intended as a substitute for the advice of health care professionals.

Alcoholics Anonymous, AA, and the Big Book are registered trademarks of Alcoholics Anonymous World Services, Inc.

Excerpts from *Narcotics Anonymous* were reprinted by permission of NA World Services, Inc. All rights reserved.

16 15 14 13   1 2 3 4 5 6

Cover design: Terri Kinne
Interior design: Kinne Design
Typesetting: BookMobile Design & Digital Publisher Services

Editor's Note

This book summarizes the combined experiences of various people in recovery and the current research and practices in the fields of addiction science and treatment. Our goal was to bring together the best thinking we could find on recovery from addiction to alcohol and other drugs. This book does not claim to speak for the organizations mentioned in these pages or any other recovery group or treatment facility, including the Hazelden Foundation, Alcoholics Anonymous, or Narcotics Anonymous. The opinions and ideas presented about these and other treatment and Twelve Step recovery programs, and the basic texts they have published, are those of the people who were the sources for the content herein. We recommend that people in any of these Twelve Step programs use the textbooks and other conference-approved materials published by these organizations as their basic guides to recovery. The stories in this book are based on the experiences of real people, but the names and some identifying information have been changed to protect their anonymity. Some of the stories are composites of two or more people's experiences to better illustrate a point in the text.

Contents

What This Book Is About

It's hard to ignore the presence of alcohol and other drugs in the world around us. We see whiskey bottles on billboards and more beer commercials than we can count when watching sports on TV. We hear news stories about superstars getting arrested for cocaine possession or drunken driving or hear how medical marijuana can help people who have diseases. We see how alcohol, marijuana, cigarettes, and other drug use is glamorized on television or in the movies, or we go to a favorite restaurant and notice how many people are enjoying a cocktail or a beer or glass of wine with their dinners. Alcohol and other drugs are a fact of life.

It's also a fact that most people who drink or use drugs can stop when they want to with no obvious problems. Others who use alcohol or marijuana once in a while might be able to control their use or stop altogether when they run into trouble. Still others might even experiment with a powerful drug like heroin once or twice and not get addicted to it. There are some of us, though, who can't control our drinking or drug use no matter how hard we try or how much it hurts us or the people we care about.

Even though it might be hard to believe, there are millions of people just like us all over the world—people who are addicted to alcohol or other drugs. No matter how low we may have sunk or how out of control our drinking or drugging has become, we are not alone. There are a growing number of us who have found a way to break free from the vise-like grip addiction had on our lives. This may mean that we escaped the hardship of life on the streets because of a $400-a-day heroin habit. Or we simply escaped living a life of lies—our families still seemed to be together and we held on to our job even while hiding the increasing amounts of alcohol it took for us to get through a day. This book describes what we've learned about addiction and what we did when we realized the damage alcohol and other drugs was doing to us and to the people in our lives. We wrote this book for people like us who think—or who know—that their drinking or drug use is out of control. Our wish is that they will find help and hope in these pages.

Mind-altering drugs have caused trouble throughout history, but it's only been in the recent past that scientists figured out why so many of us get hooked on them. Drugs like opium and cocaine, for example, were once used for both pleasure and to relieve pain. Some doctors actually used to prescribe cocaine for patients who were depressed. Now we know how drugs like cocaine can become addictive. Alcohol, which causes more problems than all other drugs combined, usually isn't even thought of as a drug. Neither is tobacco. And after alcohol and marijuana, addiction to prescription pain-killers (which are opioids, like morphine and heroin) is the third most common addiction.

The pieces of the addiction puzzle began to fall into place with the founding of Alcoholics Anonymous (AA) in the 1930s. Until that time, we didn't really know much about alcoholism. Many people believed it was a weakness of will or a sin. (Unfortunately, some people still think that way.) In 1939, AA founders published *Alcoholics Anonymous,* or the Big Book, the basic text for their members. The Big Book told the world what they had long known: Alcoholism is not something we choose or a condition we have because we are weak or bad. It is an illness that we can learn to manage. Today, the Big Book has been translated into forty-three different languages and is one of the best-selling books of all times.

Following AA's lead and seeing its success as a program of recovery, some who were addicted to drugs other than alcohol (or in addition to alcohol) also began getting together for mutual strength and fellowship. They realized they couldn't control their drug use alone, just like alcoholics couldn't control their drinking by themselves. They discovered that the Twelve Steps of AA offered a path to recovery for them too. In 1953, Narcotics Anonymous (NA) was formed, and in 1962 they published their own basic text.

In 1954, the New York City Medical Society on Alcoholism officially said that alcoholism was a disease. This was an important step that launched our present-day field of addiction medicine and research. Since then there have been great advances in understanding what addiction is, how to treat it, and what it takes to recover from it long term.

We now know that whether our drug of choice is alcohol, prescription drugs, or illegal drugs, there are some of us who can't use any mood-altering chemicals like other people. When we continue to use them, our bodies get out of balance, and our need to use grows stronger than ever. What we do to fill that need messes up our thinking and changes how we see the world. When anything affects both our bodies and our minds like this, it also affects our spirits—that larger sense of belonging and purpose we all need to succeed and grow in life. Addiction, then, is a disorder of the body, mind, and spirit—of the whole person. Things like a bad or good childhood or relationship, a hard or easy life, being rich or poor, popular or not, can make it harder or easier to abuse drugs—or stop using them when they cause problems. But none of those things alone will cause or cure addiction. Some of us have a disorder that affects the way our bodies react to drugs—a disorder that has such a hold on us that we risk losing everything, including our lives, if we don't stop drinking or drugging.

We can understand the physical part of addiction better if we compare it to an allergy. While most people can eat peanuts without worry, people with a severe peanut allergy cannot. Their bodies respond differently and treat the proteins in the peanuts as harmful invaders. They can have serious reactions and even die when they come in contact with or eat peanuts. Similarly, for some of us, the chemicals in alcohol and other drugs are the invaders that cause our bodies to react in ways that are different from people without addiction. Alcoholism was even called an allergy by Dr. William Silkworth in 1939 when he wrote one of the first parts of the Big Book, called "The Doctor's Opinion." While we know today that the abnormal reaction alcoholics and addicts have to mood-altering chemicals isn't an allergy, Silkworth was the first medical professional to call alcoholism a physical disorder, which laid the foundation for treating addiction as a disease.

Dr. Silkworth also said that addiction was a psychological (both mental and emotional) disorder that fools us into thinking we can control how much or how often we drink or use. Addiction affects our minds by trying to convince us that *this* time will be different; *this* time we'll stop before we pass out or get so high we don't know what we're doing—or we can't remember what we've done. We might even be able to control our drinking or drug use for a time. But as millions of alcoholics and addicts have learned the hard way, addiction is a chronic and ever-present disease that will only get worse if we keep drinking or using. It's also a fatal disease unless we find a way to quit and stay quit.

We come to these pages at different stages in our journeys. Some of us may think, "My drinking or drugging isn't *that* bad," but still we're a little curious and want to learn more about addiction. Others of us may have thought about cutting down on how much we drink or use drugs, or we've even thought about quitting, and we'd like to learn more about how to do either. And then there are those of us who know we need to change our lives, and we're ready to find help and guidance—or we may have already begun a program of recovery.

It doesn't matter who we are or what stage we're at. It doesn't matter if we are trying to quit drinking or using for the first time or the fifth. To get the most out of this book, all we need is the willingness to open ourselves to the possibility of a new and better life.

The "Now" in the title of this book has two meanings. First, it means that the information we're sharing about addiction and recovery is up-to-date. But it also tells us that we can begin recovery by simply deciding to stop drinking and using other drugs *today*. We don't have to worry about tomorrow or next week or next year; we decide to stop, just for today. And then tomorrow we make the same decision, and we continue to make that decision each day, one day at a time.

The book begins with a letter from Dr. Marvin Seppala, who describes addiction from both a professional and a personal perspective. In the first four chapters, we learn about telling our stories as a way to understand our relationship to alcohol and other drugs. Then we look more closely at what we mean when we say that addiction is a chronic disorder of the body, mind, and spirit. The rest of this book offers a proven program of recovery that will help us find a life free from alcohol and other drugs. Those of us who have thoroughly applied these principles in our lives are no longer obsessed by mood-altering chemicals. Instead, our "one day at a time" becomes a life of freedom and self-respect. In the last chapter, we learn about the different types of recovery groups that are available today. This chapter also describes what happens at a typical recovery meeting.

This book is for anyone interested in learning more about addiction, no matter what your personal background, gender, culture, age, or religious beliefs. *Recovery Now* combines the wisdom of programs like AA and NA with the time-tested ideas and practices that both addiction professionals and everyday people in recovery have discovered since those programs were founded. This book is not meant to replace AA's

Big Book or the NA text, but to serve as a companion and gateway to their timeless messages. If you join or belong to AA, NA, or another Twelve Step group, it's best to use the basic text of that program as your recovery guide.

We invite you to keep an open mind as you explore whether recovery is for you. Bill W., the cofounder of AA, said it best in the foreword to the Big Book of AA: *Yet it is our great hope that all those who have as yet found no answer may begin to find one in the pages of this book and will presently join us on the high road to a new freedom.*[1]

---

1. *Alcoholics Anonymous,* 4th ed. (New York: Alcoholics Anonymous World Services, 2001), xxi.

A Doctor Looks at Addiction

I have devoted my career to the treatment of alcoholism and drug addiction, but my first exposure to Twelve Step programs was when I was in treatment myself after dropping out of high school at age seventeen. I continued to use drugs and alcohol for eighteen months after treatment but eventually found my way to a Twelve Step meeting, and I've been sober for more than thirty-seven years. All of my higher educational experiences came after I got into recovery. My original plan was to become a surgeon until halfway through medical school, when I discovered how unlikely it was for doctors to diagnose people with addiction disorders let alone refer them for appropriate treatment. So instead of becoming a surgeon, I finished medical school and completed a residency in psychiatry and a fellowship in addiction medicine. I am currently the chief medical officer of a major national addiction treatment organization, the same one I attended in my youth. I am one of those grateful alcoholics and addicts you may have heard about. Twelve Step programs saved my life, gave me a blueprint for living, and provided me with an incredible career.

A tremendous amount of research has now proven that addiction is a chronic disease of the brain—which is what the founders of AA first said in the late 1930s. Despite this knowledge, many people, including some health care professionals, still describe addiction as some sort of moral weakness or failure of the will. ("She just can't hold her liquor," or, "Why doesn't he just stop?"). We now know that an addiction disorder is *not* caused by a lack of willpower; it is *not* the result of anyone's lifestyle choices, and it is *not* some form of personal weakness. Neither is addiction the result of a certain personality type, and it isn't caused by certain mental illnesses (although having a mental illness does increase the risk for addiction). As this book explains, addiction is a chronic brain disorder that affects our bodies, our minds, and our spirits.

The risk factors for addiction are like many other illnesses. Addiction can run in families, just like height and hair color, with genes being the number one risk factor for addiction. If one of your parents has an addiction disorder, you are up to six times more likely to develop one yourself. Addiction is also more common in certain cultures than in others. Someone with a high-inherited risk for addiction may only need to try alcohol or opioids (a drug class that includes some prescription painkillers and heroin) once and they begin craving regular use that moves quickly into active addiction. However, many other things might have to come into play for someone with a low-inherited risk to become addicted. The family you grow up in can shape your understanding and choices regarding addictive substances. For example, families that have relaxed views of alcohol and drug use and who use drugs and alcohol freely have a higher risk of addiction. And we now know that the younger we begin using, the greater our risk for addiction becomes. Just as having a psychiatric illness increases your risk of substance use that leads to addiction, so too does having a history of traumatic experiences (like rape or assault). Because we can't alter our genes, most of us with an addiction disorder need to do whatever we can to raise our children in a way that limits the other risk factors for them. Those of us who have found a program that helps us stay sober so we can raise our children in a loving, stable home are grateful that we're learning ways to reduce some of the risks for addiction in our families.

As this book explains in chapter 2, an addiction disorder affects the way our brains send and receive messages. Addiction disorders negatively affect the primitive part of our brain called the "reward center" because it rewards those behaviors that keep us alive from one generation to the next (like eating and sex) with a chemical called dopamine that produces feelings of pleasure. Drug abuse over time also harms the part of our brain called the prefrontal cortex. This is the part we use to think and plan for the future and to work toward a certain goal. In other words, this is the part of the brain that tells us when we have a problem and how to solve it. When our brains tell us that the pleasure of getting drunk or high is just as important—maybe even more important—than survival activities like eating and having sex, it rewards us when we actually do drink alcohol or take drugs by producing more and more of the "feel-good" chemical dopamine. Since this thinking and problem-solving part of our brain isn't working right, we don't even see that our overwhelming desire and need for alcohol and drugs is a problem. How can we be expected to solve a problem if we don't even know one exists? Yet many people expect us to do just that—they think we can simply use our willpower to quit using alcohol and drugs on our own. They don't understand that our brains have been fooled into acting as if the most important thing in our lives is to get high, even if we die trying.

I knew a nurse with a heroin addiction disorder who was in a gas station bathroom without running water. She used toilet water to cook up her heroin for injection. I know of an anesthesiologist who dumped out the "sharps box" where patients and doctors throw away dirty needles and broken vials, all of which could carry dangerous infections. He sifted through the contents with his bare hands hoping to find a container with a few drops of fentanyl, an extremely powerful opioid. I know an alcoholic man who pulled out his IVs and drainage tubes shortly after a major abdominal surgery in order to walk down the street in his hospital gown to have a few drinks. I also met a single mother with such a serious methamphetamine addiction disorder that, when she ran into her dealer on the way to the grocery store, she didn't buy groceries at all. Instead, she ended up going with him on a four-day trip to score meth. Her children, both under the age of five, were taken away by the Department of Human Services to be cared for by someone else. This mom didn't love her children any less than I love mine; she was driven by something even more powerful than the survival of her own children—her addiction disorder.

As we learn more about how alcohol and drugs affect the brain, we find that some addiction disorders can be treated with medications. Although some people still find this controversial, I agree with the majority of treatment professionals who support using these meds to help with cravings when it is appropriate to do so. Addiction is a disease that calls for the best that science has to offer. The medications approved by the U.S. Food and Drug Administration (FDA) for alcoholism are nonaddictive and can be of help to some people. There are also FDA-approved medications that doctors prescribe for people who are dependent on opioids like heroin and some prescription painkillers. These medications can be lifesaving, and we should consider using them as a way to reduce the high number of deaths from overdose and infections from IV drug use. Someday we might even discover a medication that can guarantee abstinence from addictive drugs. But even if that day comes, those of us with addiction disorders will still need what Twelve Step recovery programs offer: healing of mind and spirit and support for the journey. Again, this is true whether or not we use prescribed medications to help deal with cravings and withdrawal.

How can a program of action such as the Twelve Steps—which talks about love, service, spirituality, and a higher power—treat a disease that affects the body and mind as well as the spirit? Brain scanning studies show that when we experience love and spirituality (however we each define those terms), the same "feel good" chemicals are released as when we use alcohol and drugs. How many places can an active addict or alcoholic experience this besides at a Twelve Step meeting, where they are likely to be welcomed, hugged, and told they are the most important person in the room? People in active addiction or in early recovery need a great deal of help and unconditional acceptance, and many find this at recovery meetings. Our families and friends have watched us wreck our lives during active addiction. By the time we enter recovery, we have often worn out our welcome with them, and they have a hard time putting all that behind them and supporting us completely. But at most Twelve Step recovery meetings we can find the support we need. We know that what we say in meetings stays in meetings and that our confidentiality and anonymity are protected. We find a community of caring people who will take our calls at 3:00 a.m., listen to our list of excuses, and still ask us to join them for dinner or coffee. Spirituality—a personal sense of a power greater than self, however we experience that power—is at the heart of Twelve Step recovery, and the Steps specifically provide a path to wholeness and life change not only for our body and mind, but also for our spirit. Love and spirituality directly speak to the "reward center" in our brains in a way that appears to heal even the most broken among us.

As a physician, even with my own recovery experience, I want to know what the research studies show before referring my patients to any treatment for an addiction disorder. I am happy to report that an increasing number of high-quality research studies show that addiction treatment and Twelve Step recovery is effective. For example, one study found that people were twice as likely to remain abstinent from alcohol and other drugs if they attended AA or other Twelve Step groups after treatment versus those who only go to treatment. Another study revealed that people who attend AA after treatment were more than twice as likely to be sober at one year and also at three years after treatment. Several other studies show that the more AA or other Twelve Step meetings you attend, the more likely you are to stay sober.

However, research also tells us that attending a recovery group is not enough; people also need to get actively involved in working a recovery program to stay sober. Having a sponsor, engaging in Twelve Step work, leading a meeting, sponsoring others, and working all the Steps in order also affects abstinence. When people attend meetings and see how many others can stay sober, they start to believe they can do the same, and this new confidence helps them do just that. Working a recovery program also improves our coping skills, which helps us handle the day-to-day challenges of life outside of recovery.

When I was in treatment in 1974, I was told that addiction is a disease, but I wasn't told what that meant. My addiction didn't seem like a disease; it seemed like something I had done to myself and to everyone around me. I carried enormous shame and guilt about how I had mistreated my family. The remorse I felt about my dishonesty, my thefts, the way I had quit sports and dropped out of high school, was overwhelming. I felt as though I were pure evil and unable to get along well with most other people. My only relief seemed to come from using drugs and alcohol. Would I have stayed sober right after treatment had I known what research now proves—that addiction is a disorder of the body, mind, and the spirit? Who knows, but I probably would not have blamed myself for as long as I did.

A few years ago, I gave a lecture to patients at a treatment program on the same night as a graduation event for people who had successfully completed their treatment program. I described how addiction affects our brains and our behavior, much like I've done here. Afterward, many of the patients and their families told me my talk made so much sense to them and they found it helpful to have addiction explained that way. Then I went to the graduation where each graduate described what was of most help to them during their treatment experience. They mentioned their counselors, their peers, the role of starting a Twelve Step program, and spirituality. These were emotional, heartfelt accounts of the tremendous changes they had experienced. Not one person mentioned brain science.

Knowledge of this disease is helpful, but that alone won't keep us sober. Bill Wilson and the other early AAers recognized the importance of telling people that addiction is a disease. That's why they chose to highlight the disease aspect of alcoholism by placing "The Doctor's Opinion" at the front of AA's Big Book, *Alcoholics Anonymous*. We know today that what's true for alcoholism is true for addiction to other drugs as well. Those pioneers also knew how important it was to emphasize that addiction is a mental and spiritual disorder as well as a physical disorder, the solution for which can be found in working a recovery program like the Twelve Steps and finding mutual support with other alcoholics and addicts. I am grateful today to know that I have a disease of the body, mind, and spirit that I can manage a day at a time by living my life based on this simple solution. I hope this book helps you find a similar solution and a way to live a full life in recovery.

Marvin D. Seppala, M.D.
May 2013

Our Relationship with Alcohol and Other Drugs

We know and understand each other—and ourselves—through the stories we tell about our lives. When it comes to our drinking or other drug use, the stories we tell ourselves can keep us in denial that we have a problem. Or, if we're honest in the telling, our stories can move us to take a closer look at our use and its impact on ourselves and others. We also learn about ourselves from listening to each other's stories. This is why over two-thirds of both AA's textbook, *Alcoholics Anonymous* or the Big Book, and the Narcotics Anonymous basic text are filled with stories of how people recognized, faced, and then dealt with their various addictions. It's also why many AA and NA meetings feature speakers who share their stories.

Bill W., the cofounder of AA, relapsed several times and ended up in the hospital near death before he was finally able to stay sober. He had come to accept that alcoholism was a disease and understood at last that his willpower alone was no match for it. He had a spiritual experience that restored him to sanity and, as a result, he believed that a relationship with a higher power was the solution for his illness. Once sober, he tried to tell other alcoholics what they should do to get sober, but that didn't work. No one likes to be told what to do, especially alcoholics and addicts. Later, when he honestly shared his personal story of alcoholism and recovery with Dr. Bob, a physician from Akron, Ohio, he was actually able to help someone else quit drinking. Bill was on a business trip to Akron when his cravings for alcohol became so strong that he knew he was in trouble. He figured he had two choices: go to the hotel bar and get loaded or call another alcoholic for help. Desperate, he found the phone number of an area minister who put him in touch with some people who led him to Dr. Bob, who was known to have a serious drinking problem. The two men ended up talking for hours, and Bill W. and Dr. Bob became the cofounders of AA.

At this first meeting, Bill simply talked about his history with alcohol, the repeated binges followed by hospitalizations and promises to quit, and how he had lost his career and had almost lost his marriage and his very life. He then told Dr. Bob about how he faced his powerlessness over alcohol by seeking help from a higher power. Bill was amazed when Dr. Bob listened with such great interest. As he listened,

Dr. Bob thought about his own out-of-control drinking and saw himself in Bill. A month later, he got sober too. When the two men decided to share their message of addiction and recovery with a third alcoholic, they discovered what was later to become the heart of AA: one drunk helping another.

. . .

Most of us are good at telling stories, but if we're abusing alcohol and other drugs, we often tell tales and shade the truth to cover up or justify our use. We get good at explaining away our drinking and drugging by telling ourselves and others things like, "I only drink and get high because I'm stressed." Or, "Everybody I know drinks and does drugs, and I'm no worse than them." Or maybe we compare ourselves to someone in much worse shape than we are as proof that *we're* not all that bad.

We also find other reasons for the physical problems that stem from our drinking or using: Our morning headache and nausea is probably the flu (not a hangover). Our weight loss is because of a diet (not our increased cocaine or meth use). Our lack of motivation and drive is because our job or school isn't rewarding (and not related to our daily marijuana use). This line of thinking makes sense to us, especially in the early stages of addiction when it's hard to tell the difference between social use and problem use. And we can probably convince others who are concerned about our drinking or drugging that we don't have a problem. Our explanations usually work for a while. We may even believe the stories we tell others and ourselves because our lives and our drug use may still seem manageable. But when we cross that blurry line from "I want to drink and use" to "I *need* to drink and use," we often discover that those stories no longer fit. This is how it was for Jane.

> To my friends and coworkers, I was the picture of success. I was the only woman executive in a thriving high-tech company. I had a good marriage and a teenage son who was doing well in school. I worked long hours and so looked forward to unwinding at the end of each day with a glass of wine or a beer, either at home or at a local bar's happy hour. I have always worried about fitting in, and in high school I discovered that smoking a little marijuana helped take the edge off—a practice I carried with me into adulthood. On the way home from one of my many happy hour gatherings, I got arrested for driving under the influence of both alcohol and pot. When the judge gave me the choice of losing my license or going to recovery meetings as part of my probation, I figured I had to jump through the hoops and go to the meetings with a bunch of addicts who I wouldn't

have a thing in common with. But something happened to me when I went to those meetings. Week after week, I listened—*really* listened—to people's stories of why they were there. I began to see myself in their words, and I began to look at my life and my drug use more honestly. When it came time for me to share, the story that came out was different from the story I had been telling myself for years. I realized I had more than a drink or two every night and had been doing more than "a little" marijuana. I had a drug problem and needed help.

Jane decided to see an addictions specialist to get a formal assessment of her drinking and marijuana use. This evaluation identified the following signs of a substance use disorder and confirmed what Jane thought: She was addicted.

- TOLERANCE—it took more and more alcohol and marijuana to get the same high she got when she first started using.

- WITHDRAWAL—she experienced physical and psychological (mental and emotional) discomfort when she hadn't used for a time (which can be different for different people and different drugs).

- LOSS OF CONTROL—she was having trouble limiting how much or how often she used.

- HARMFUL CONSEQUENCES—she was unable to stop using despite many attempts to quit, even when she knew she could get in trouble.
- PREOCCUPATION—she spent a great deal of time thinking about using, planning her next drunk or high, making sure there would be plenty of alcohol at parties, and scoring her marijuana.

Like Jane, we find that our personal stories can do more than give us the information we need to honestly assess our drug use. Our stories can help us make sense of who we are, where we've been, and where we might be heading. If, like Jane, we decide to get serious about quitting drinking or drugging, we learn to tell our stories by honestly describing

- what it was like when we were using
- what happened to make us realize we might have a problem
- what it's like now that we've stopped using and have decided to get help

When we listen with an open mind and without judgment, we can also learn from other people's stories of addiction and recovery. Often we will hear something in someone else's story that is exactly what we needed to know for whatever stage we're at in understanding the impact that alcohol and other drugs have had on our lives.

At first, we might find it hard to even picture ourselves going to a recovery meeting because we see our using-related behaviors as shameful or as a sign of weakness. It certainly isn't easy to let other people see that part of ourselves, especially if we've been told since childhood to hide our "dirty laundry." Yet, those of us who have made the decision to get help find that we're not alone. When we attend Twelve Step recovery meetings and treatment programs, we find that other people had lives just as unmanageable as ours had become and that they found support and help from other alcoholics and addicts. We learn that we're not at fault for having the disease of addiction, but we are responsible for doing something about it. AA, NA, and other peer support meetings are held in every major city around the world and in most towns of any size. Some of us were curious about what happens in a meeting, and we found it helpful to go to a few meetings and just listen to the stories that were being told there—the stories of other alcoholics and addicts. We may have known somebody already in recovery and asked that person to take us to a meeting. Some of us called information or looked up AA or NA meetings on the Internet and just showed up at one. We were relieved to find out that we could attend meetings and participate at whatever level was comfortable for us, including just listening. (For more about Twelve Step and other peer support meetings, turn to chapter 11, where we discuss such peer recovery groups in more detail.)

Sometimes we hear stories like Rafael's. Like so many of our stories, his isn't a pretty one. He lived high, partied hard, and lost almost everything because of his addiction. Fear, he said, sobered him up for a while, but it wasn't enough to keep him sober over the long term. His story shows how powerful addiction can be, but we also see that no matter how hard our lives are and whatever the toll drugs have taken, change is possible and we can recover. Rafael did eventually quit using and stayed drug free long enough to build a new life. Here's his story.

> I grew up in a tough, inner-city neighborhood where drugs were a way of life. I smoked so much weed as a kid that my friends used to call me Hash. Then I tried crack and heroin and loved the rush I got from them. But those habits cost money, so I started stealing—first from my mom's purse, then from neighbors and local stores. Pretty soon, I started dealing drugs myself. I was a mess, and some nights I'd come home late at night to hear my mom crying herself to sleep. I knew I was breaking her heart, so I left home and crashed with whoever had room. I

knew the local cops had their eyes on me, but I was careful not to speed or carry any drugs in my car. If I got pulled over, I'd act polite but pissed, asking if I was being stopped for "driving while Hispanic." One night I overdosed on heroin and my "friends" left me for dead. At least one of them thought to call 911 after they took off, and I got taken to the hospital and put in detox. The doc who treated me—a big tough-looking dude—told me I almost died. Then he said, "I almost killed myself with drugs, too, when I was a teenager, but my parents got me into treatment. You don't have to live like this." He hooked me up with the drug counselor at the hospital, and they helped get me into a treatment program and halfway house. It took a while, but I go to NA meetings regularly and am clean now—one day at a time.

Even after hearing stories like Jane's and Rafael's, some of us don't believe we have the same problem they did with alcohol and drugs. We may think our stories are unique because our circumstances are different from the "average" alcoholic or other drug addict. We think *our* lives can't compare to theirs because we're gay or black or a woman or young or old or poor or rich and successful or we grew up on a reservation. But if we admit that we might be addicted, we discover that even though our lives and stories are different,

our situation is the same: Our drinking and drug use is causing problems in our lives that we haven't been able to solve
on our own and we may need help.

Before we get to that point, though, it's common for us to
still think that we can control our use or quit whenever we
want to. If that's true of you, we suggest you try telling your
story anyway just to see if you learn anything new. We have
found it helps to start by writing out our stories in as much
detail as possible, describing what our alcohol and other
drug use has been like, what's happened because of it, and
where we are with it right now. If you don't like to write and
you can find a recorder or computer with voice recognition,
tell your story as if you're talking to someone you trust completely. When we do this, we start from the beginning and
are as honest as we can be. We try to include all the things
that might be connected to our drug use, like losing a job,
getting arrested, losing friends, or having trouble in relationships. Our problems might not be that extreme, but if we are
thorough and truthful, we are likely to discover ways that
our use was harmful.

After we write or record our stories, it often helps to actually share them with someone we can trust (for example, a
drug counselor, therapist, or doctor who understands addiction; a clergyperson; a trusted friend or relative; or someone in AA or NA). We should choose someone who will not

tell our stories to other people and who will listen to them objectively, without having an opinion about them. Telling our true stories to ourselves and others is a way for us to begin to take responsibility for our actions and get the help we need if we realize our drinking and drugging is a problem. When we share our stories with someone else, we try to remember to do so with no expectations. We share because we want to get at our deeper truths about the impact of our drug-using behavior.

We know from experience that it can be exhausting to keep our worries, our fears, or our truths about our drug use inside of us. And it's just as hard to try to cover up or hide our use if we know we have a problem. Many of us find great relief when we name our fears and share our real story with someone who understands—it's like a great weight is lifted. When we risk letting someone see us as we really are—and that person listens, understands, and accepts us—we can begin to accept the truth about ourselves.

. . .

If you try these suggestions and find that you want to know more about addiction, keep reading. We will look more closely at addiction in the next three chapters and learn why it's called a disorder of the body, mind, and spirit.

Walt Disney once said, "We keep moving forward, opening

new doors, and doing new things, because we're curious and curiosity keeps leading us down new paths." But it's hard to open new doors if our minds are closed or to explore new paths if we're convinced we already know the way or think we have all the answers. We encourage you to bring a spirit of open mindedness and a willingness to explore new ideas as you continue on in this book. In this way, you might see ideas that apply to you and your story.

2

Addiction Is a Disorder of the Body

What a relief it must have been for AA cofounder Bill W. when his doctor explained in the 1930s that alcoholism was an illness. In the doctor's opinion, Bill had an "allergy" to alcohol. What a relief it *is,* more than seventy-five years later, to learn that those of us who are addicted to alcohol or other drugs have a disorder that can be diagnosed and treated. Plus, science has now found that there are biological reasons why we react to drugs differently than people who don't have our illness.

Mental health professionals use the American Psychiatric Association's *Diagnostic and Statistical Manual* (the *DSM*) to help diagnose their patients' various psychological conditions. In the *DSM,* problems with alcohol and other drugs are called "substance use disorders." This category is further broken down by drug type, such as "alcohol-use disorder" or "cannabis-use disorder." The degree to which a disorder affects our life and behavior helps to determine how mild or how serious a problem is and whether or not we have a substance use disorder. (The fifth edition of the *DSM* doesn't use the term "addiction" but acknowledges that it is still commonly used by professionals, and we've chosen to use it in this book.) Some people can have lots of trouble because of their alcohol and drug use—including legal, personal, and social problems—and still be able to quit on their own when they want to. These people do not have an addiction disorder.

The National Institute on Drug Abuse (NIDA) defines addiction as "a chronic, relapsing brain disease that is characterized by compulsive drug seeking and use, despite harmful consequences."[1] What NIDA doesn't say here is that addiction is not only chronic, but without the right help, it can also be fatal. Even when the negative consequences are piling up and we risk losing everything, those of us who are addicted will keep drinking or using until we either finally decide to get help or die. Like Jane's experience in the previous chapter, we will develop tolerance (it will take more of the drug to create the same high) and our physical need for our drug of choice will grow stronger if we keep using. The more we use, the more we need. This is because of the way that alcohol and other drugs affect our brains, which, as

---

1. U.S. Department of Health and Human Services, National Institutes of Health, National Institute on Drug Abuse, *Drugs, Brains, and Behavior: The Science of Addiction* (Rockville, MD: DHHS, 2010). NIH publication no. 10-5605. Available at www.drugabuse.gov/publications /science-addiction.

Dr. Seppala pointed out in the foreword, is different from the way it affects the brains of people who aren't addicts.

Our brains have millions of cells that "talk" to each other by sending out and receiving natural chemicals. These chemicals then affect the way we think, feel, and behave. Alcohol, prescription medications, and street drugs are also chemicals. (For more about the different drugs of abuse and their effects, see appendix B). They work in the brain by tapping into this communication system and interfering with the way our cells normally send, receive, and process information. Most addictive drugs (including nicotine, one of the most addictive drugs) find their way to our brain's pleasure, or reward, center where they flood it with *dopamine*—a "feel good" chemical in the parts of the brain that control movement, emotions, thinking, motivation, and feelings of pleasure. This rush of dopamine is what causes us to feel high. It's important to know that dopamine is also released during normal positive experiences in our lives, such as when we laugh, exercise, or have sex. Some addictive drugs can release two to ten times the amount of dopamine we normally produce. When this happens over and over again, our brains try to balance things by making less natural dopamine. This means that our normal positive experiences no longer make us feel quite so good. Now we need drugs to get our dopamine level back to normal—and even more drugs to get high again. *Our brains have been hijacked.* When we don't have drugs in our system, the discomfort of withdrawal (such as intense anxiety, sweating, distorted thinking, and so on) tells us we need more drugs just to feel normal. It's a bit different when it comes to nicotine products. Although we don't get a typical drug high from smoking a cigarette or chewing tobacco, when we are addicted to it and then stop using it, we feel depressed or irritable. When our bodies get chemically out of balance like this, our need to use gets more powerful even when we want to quit.

. . .

When addiction professionals describe addiction as "chronic and relapsing," they mean that it is always with us, even after we stop using alcohol or other drugs. This doesn't make sense at first. We think, "If I can quit using for a while and start to get my life back on track, then I should be able to have a beer with my friends or snort a line at a party because I can control my using now." But that's not reality for alcoholics and addicts. It would be like someone with a peanut allergy thinking, "I should be able to have that candy bar with nuts now since I haven't had peanuts for months," or a diabetic thinking, "I should be able to have a piece of cake today because I haven't had a diabetic reaction for a while." This type of thinking could lead to dangerous or deadly results for people with food allergies or diabetes.

Just as their body chemistries are different, our brain chemistries are different in the way that they process mood-altering chemicals—no matter how long we've gone without them. If we relapse and have that drink or line, our craving will get even stronger, and our brains will tell us we need more. We alcoholics and addicts often need to find this out the hard way, which is why relapse is so common with this illness.

Relapse isn't just the actual act of taking a drink or using a drug after a period of being clean and sober. Relapse is a process that starts with warning signs that build up before that first "slip" happens. Not all of us in recovery relapse. Some might have a slip, where we relapse briefly and then quickly go back to recovery and move on to enjoy long-term abstinence. Still others of us have a full relapse and return to drinking or using like we used to. Those of us in early recovery are especially at risk for relapse. All the physical and emotional changes we are going through cause lots of stress, and we may not have had enough time to learn and practice good coping skills. Plus, our brains may be clouded by years of using substances.

If we slip or relapse, it's important to see it as just a temporary setback so we can get back to the work of recovery. One way to prevent relapse is to keep an eye out for the situations that may threaten our sobriety. Here are some dangerous situations in early recovery:

- keeping alcohol and drugs in our apartment or house
- difficult emotions like anger, anxiety, grief, and fear
- stress; tension with friends, coworkers, or family
- boredom
- isolation—being alone too much
- hanging out with people who are drinking or using
- celebrations or emotional events
- being in places or around things like advertising that remind us of using
- thinking that we can use "just a little"

We can't avoid all high-risk situations, but we can create a plan to deal with them when they do come up. We can talk with our sponsor (someone with at least two years of sobriety who has agreed to guide us in our program of recovery), a trusted family member or friend, or our recovery group about ways to leave a "sticky" situation, ways to practice positive "self-talk," and how we can deal with difficult feelings. We can also agree that if we feel like we might relapse or if we have relapsed, we will immediately call our sponsor or someone we trust and get the help we need.

As many of us who have been in recovery for some time know all too well, we also risk relapse when we get lazy about our recovery work. We might let our guard down or think we have more control than we really do in high-risk situations. We might think, "This time it will be different," and have a drink, but our brains and bodies aren't satisfied with just one drink. They're saying, "That isn't enough—we need more." This is what Mel discovered.

Alcohol was my drug of choice. I began abusing it when I was in the service and stationed on the island of Guam during World War II. Much to the envy of my fellow marines, I became the regular bartender in the officer's club, where I had easy access to all the booze I wanted. After the war, I returned to my home in Michigan, and I brought my love of booze with me. I married my high school sweetheart, and our life resembled a 1950s movie: three kids, a house in the suburbs, and cocktails every night when I came home from the office. On the weekends, our house was the place to be, and I was the hit of every party.

Over the next twenty years, my drinking got more and more out of hand. My kids stayed clear of me, and my friends started making excuses not to come over. Every time I tried to quit drinking, I eventually fell off the wagon. I started missing so much work that my boss gave me an ultimatum: dry up or get fired. Feeling desperate, my wife phoned Jim, a friend of ours who belonged to AA. I finally agreed to get help and went to meetings faithfully, practiced my recovery program, and stayed sober for twelve years—until my daughter's wedding. I was so confident that I had won my battle over alcohol, I toasted the bride and groom with champagne. Then I had a few glasses of whiskey "just to be sociable" at the reception. My drinking continued for almost a week after the wedding, and when my wife found me passed out in the living room one morning, she once again called Jim, who cleaned me up and got me into a treatment program. I started going to meetings again and have now been sober one day at a time for thirty-four years.

What Mel and other alcoholics and drug addicts might not know is that when we repeatedly drink or use other drugs in response to our craving, our brain chemistry changes in more extreme ways over time. When "normal" people have a few drinks or take a drug once in a while, changes occur in their brains that make them feel high, but the changes are in the short term—their brains return to normal once the drug is out of their system. When our addicted brains are repeatedly exposed to drugs, including alcohol, the chemistry changes stay in place, and over time, we need more drugs to get high.

Today, brain scans show how just the thought of drugs makes addicts want to use them. In one study involving cocaine addicts in recovery and people with no history of drug use, researchers did brain scans on both groups while showing them videos of drug-related items. The brains of the recovering cocaine addicts lit up while the videos played— revealing an increase in the dopamine levels in the pleasure centers of their brains. The brains of the nonaddicts did not respond to the videos. Even though the cocaine addicts had stopped using drugs, they still craved them.

As this study showed, sights, sounds, smells, and thoughts linked to our memories of using alcohol and other drugs can set off cravings that send strong messages to our body, saying, "You *need* this drug!" We can feel physically excited as our brain chemistry responds to the thought of using again. We experience a sense of intense pleasure that drowns out any warning thoughts of how bad drugs have been for us in the past. We feel a *compulsion*—a very strong urge—to drink or use.

The good news is that no matter how powerful our addiction has been or how strong our cravings may be, recovery is possible. There are a variety of treatment approaches that can help us cope with how drugs have affected our bodies and that can help us deal with our cravings. For some of us—especially those with opioid addiction and alcoholics or addicts who have severe long-term physical dependencies— there are anticraving medications that can stabilize us and even things out a little while we begin building a solid recovery program.[2]

Doctors may prescribe buprenorphine, for example, to help reduce withdrawal symptoms and cravings for opioids—especially heroin, but also prescription painkillers like Vicodin and OxyContin. It is substituted for the opioid and then use is scaled back over time. There are also a number of medications that may help with withdrawal symptoms from nicotine, like the nicotine patch, gum, lozenges, and nasal sprays and medications that do not contain nicotine. With the right help, we can be released from the grip and false promises of mood-altering chemicals.

In addition to cravings, our brains are affected in other ways when we use addictive substances for a long time. For example, we often can't remember things as well as we used to. Our judgment—our ability to tell right from wrong or to see the connection between using drugs and the bad things that result from them—can also suffer, and we get into trouble more often. We lose insight, which means we have trouble thinking clearly about our actions and reactions. More and more, we deny to ourselves and to others that we have a problem. And our brain's "reward circuitry" gets fouled up,

---

2. The three FDA-approved medications for alcohol dependence are disulfiram, acamprosate, and naltrexone. There are also three FDA-approved medications for opioid dependence: methadone, buprenorphine, and naltrexone.

so we come to believe that we can only feel good or enjoy ourselves if we drink booze or use drugs.

. . .

Mood-altering chemicals affect more than our brains. If we use often enough and long enough, other parts of our bodies suffer as well. For example, alcohol can harm most of our body's organs, like the heart, liver, and intestines. Stimulants like cocaine and methamphetamine can cause heart attacks, strokes, extreme paranoia, and memory loss. Marijuana use impairs short-term memory and learning, increases heart rate, and can harm our lungs. Use of synthetic drugs, like synthetic marijuana or chemicals called "bath salts," can result in heart attacks, seizures, strokes, high blood pressure, and psychotic symptoms that cause users to become paranoid or violent. With opioids like oxycodone and heroin, there's a high incidence of overdose and death. And when we shoot up opioids or meth, we risk serious infectious diseases, including HIV/AIDS and hepatitis C. Inhalants, like paint or glue, are extremely toxic and can damage the heart, kidneys, lungs, and brain. Even a healthy person can suffer heart failure and death within minutes of a single session of prolonged sniffing. And let's not forget about tobacco use, which is the leading preventable cause of disease, disability, and death in the United States. This is just a partial list of health risks from using alcohol and other drugs, and it doesn't include the hundreds of thousands of deaths and injuries every year from auto and other accidents, violent behavior, suicides, and overdoses that are related to addiction and drug abuse.

Although most of us probably know about the risks we've mentioned, our addiction disorder tells us that we will be the exception—it won't happen to us. Or we may say, "I'll take my chances—getting high is worth it." For some of us, though, learning that we have a treatable, physical disorder can help us accept that we need help. As Dr. Seppala points out in the foreword to this book, for many alcoholics and addicts, hearing about the research that shows that addiction, like many other physical and mental disorders, can be handed down from generation to generation helps them overcome the stigma or bad feelings about having an addiction. We know now that if someone in our families like a parent or grandparent had problems with alcohol or other drugs, we are more at risk of becoming addicted too. Studies done of twins who were raised in different adoptive households did much to help us understand how addiction can be inherited. These studies found a greater rate of alcoholism among twins who had an alcoholic biological parent, even though the twins weren't raised by their biological parents and the two children didn't grow up together.

Learning that addiction can run in families helps us understand why we might react differently to alcohol and other drugs and be more likely to become addicted than others might be. Although she was a young adult when she found out about her grandfather's history of drug addiction, KimLi was relieved to get this piece to her own "addiction puzzle." Here's her story.

> When I was in college, I got hooked on speed after one of my friends introduced me to it as a "study aid." It was great. I could stay up all night studying, get a few hours of sleep, pop another amphetamine pill, and go to class. Then I thought, "If one is good, two must be better," and started taking more. I also started experimenting with cocaine and loved the rush that gave me too. When I started having frequent headaches and nausea and a few other flu-like symptoms, I decided to go to the campus health center. By that time, my grades were slipping—I just couldn't seem to remember what I'd studied long enough to take a test, but I figured it was because I was feeling so crummy. When the doctor I saw asked me about drug use, I told her I took speed "once in a while" but said it wasn't a problem— everybody did that. I didn't mention the coke, but I think she suspected I wasn't telling her the whole story. Then she started asking me questions about

cravings and tolerance and what happens when I didn't use amphetamines—like when I go home on break. I answered her questions, and I was floored when she said, "It looks to me like you have a drug problem." She referred me to the school addiction specialist, who diagnosed me with an addiction.

My parents are absolute teetotalers, who never drank and who don't even like to take aspirin. My brother and the cousins I knew never drank or took drugs either, so my diagnosis was truly a surprise to me. When I worked up the courage to tell my parents that I needed to go to outpatient treatment for a drug addiction, I admitted how ashamed I felt to be the only one in the family with this disease. Then my mother said, "You never knew your grandfather who lived in China, because you were a baby when he died of a drug overdose." Although I know now that I could be an addict even if I didn't have a relative who had the disease of addiction, I'm glad I have this information. When I have children, I plan to tell them how my grandfather and I were both addicted to drugs—and how they're "playing with a loaded gun" when it comes to alcohol and other drug use because of our family history. Who knows? Maybe that information will help keep them clean and sober.

As KimLi learned, when we know how drugs affect our bodies and are aware of our individual risk factors, we better understand our own addictions. And this just might help prevent our children or others from abusing drugs and falling prey to this disorder. But even having this knowledge does not guarantee that we and our children won't have to deal with addiction someday. Conditions in our environment—such as family conflict, abuse and neglect, poverty and crime, and peer pressure—can put us at risk too. As mentioned earlier, studies have shown that the younger we are when we start drinking or drugging, the faster we can become addicted. Plus, the more environmental risk factors we have—in addition to the physical factors that come into play—the more likely we are to become addicted to alcohol or other drugs.

When we look at our own stories, as we began to do in the previous chapter, we can identify our risk factors and get a clearer picture of our physical reactions and our relationship to alcohol or other drugs. It's important to know that this may be different for each addict. After all, we come from different backgrounds and we might not even react the same to the same drug. Some of us couldn't get by without alcohol, but we could take or leave marijuana or meth. Some of us went on binges of heavy drinking on weekends; others drank daily. A growing number of us stayed away from alcohol but had to have prescription painkillers or heroin to get through the day. For still others, any drug—or a combination of drugs— would do to keep us high on a regular basis.

Whatever the drug or drug combination, many of us begin to see just how little control we have over how much and how often we use. Our lives are getting more and more unmanageable because of our use, and we can't seem to gain control. When this happens, we have taken the first step in admitting that we have a problem or that we may be addicted.

. . .

Although our stories of addiction differ, as the NA text reminds us, "in the end we all have the same thing in common. This common illness or disorder is addiction. We know well the two things that make up true addiction: obsession and compulsion."[3] Among other things, we have talked about compulsion in this chapter—how our bodies will always crave alcohol or other drugs once we get used to having them in our systems. In the following chapter, we'll talk about obsession and how addiction is also a disorder of the mind.

---

3. *Narcotics Anonymous,* 6th ed. (Van Nuys, CA: Narcotics Anonymous World Services, 2008), 87.

3

Addiction Is a Disorder of the Mind

Addiction affects our minds and thoughts as well as our bodies. When we have addictive thinking, we tell ourselves things like, "I can control my drinking," or, "I can drink like any normal person," or, "I can quit anytime I want to." Some of us might even say, "I just like to drink (or use drugs). It's fun and it's an important part of my life" and "It's okay to drink what I want when I want it. It's okay to use whatever drug I want when I want it and do whatever it takes to score the drugs I need."

One of the main features of our addictive thinking is denial—the ability to turn the truth inside out and twist reality to defend our "right" to keep drinking and using, even when our lives are falling apart. We can't face the truth because that would mean we'd have to stop drinking or using. To an addict, that's like telling a starving person to go on a diet. Denial is a trick our addicted minds play on us so we can find excuses to continue our addictive behavior. It also is a way that many of us avoid facing the stigma and shame of addiction.

As many of us have experienced, even when our loved ones or bosses tell us we need to cut down or stop our drug use, we can deny having a problem. Or, we might agree that we need to cut down, so we tell them that we're going to drink only beer or smoke pot on weekends. If our using causes enough of a crisis, we might even promise to stop all together—and we may mean it at the time. But sooner or later, we'll be back to our out-of-control drinking and using. This is a sure sign of addiction. Some of us will "fall off the wagon" in a matter of hours. It could take weeks or months for others to begin using alcohol or drugs again. But as we learned in the previous chapter, addiction is a progressive disorder, which means it gets worse over time. And when we start using again after a period of abstinence, we're likely to be even more out of control than before and to experience more negative effects.

Yet, even in the face of mounting evidence that we are addicts, many of us still cling desperately to the belief that we can use alcohol or other drugs like "normal" people. It's just too painful to face the truth of our own powerlessness over how much and how often we use. To protect this belief, we might become experts at fooling even ourselves: "I never have a drink before 5:00," "I don't drink hard liquor, only beer," "I only use Ecstasy at raves because I love to dance all night," "I only snort—I never shoot up," "I need to keep taking OxyContin because my back still hurts sometimes."

When we have an addiction disorder, we often develop special tricks to convince ourselves and others that we are keeping our drinking and using under control. We may tell our spouse that our doctors weren't really helping us when they wouldn't give us any more painkillers, and then we shop around until we find a doctor who will write a prescription for us. We might hide liquor and drugs so we can have a drink or take a hit in secret. Or perhaps we have a few shots of booze or take a toke of pot in private before a social event so our use doesn't seem that bad when we're out in public. Many of us hang out only with people who drink and drug so we blend in and can justify our level of use because "Everybody else gets drunk (or high) on weekends." We may encourage our partners to drink or take drugs so we don't stand out and they can't nag us about our use. We get good at finding ways to "minimize" our problem—making it seem like it's not as bad as it is so we keep using the amount of alcohol or drugs we need to satisfy our craving.

It boils down to this: When addiction takes over our lives, we are no longer our true selves. When we look in a mirror, it's almost like we see someone else staring back at us. Both AA's Big Book and the NA text describe it as being Dr. Jekyll and Mr. Hyde—we become two people who are complete opposites of one another. The world inside ourselves and the world outside ourselves get so out of whack that we have trouble figuring out what is the actual truth and what is our twisted version of the truth. Whether we lie outright or shape the "facts" to fit what we want others (or ourselves) to believe, we find ways to deny the truth of our addiction. Jude, a man in his early twenties, told the following story as an example of how addictive thinking can work.

> I remember the time I picked up a terrible virus and was so sick for ten days that I couldn't keep anything in my stomach. I was running a temperature and just felt terrible. The only thing I could stand was water and dry toast. As much as I loved my Scotch, even the smell of whiskey made me puke when I tried to sip some. When I felt good again, I, of course, went right back to drinking. When my parents ragged on me about my drinking, I defended myself, telling them, "I just went more than a week without a drop of booze with no problem. So get off my back." I conveniently left out the part about being sick. I used the story so often as proof that I could drink normally that I started to believe it myself.

In addition to denying and reshaping reality, it is also common to think obsessively when we have an addiction disorder. When we think obsessively, we focus on one thing and one thing only. It's like nothing else is important to us. For alcoholics and addicts, using and planning the next high can take over our thoughts. Everything else—including our families, our friends, our jobs, or our health—takes a back seat to our need for drugs. Here's how Aamir, a father of four put it.

> Nothing was as important as getting and taking the drugs. "I'll deal with it tomorrow" became my constant chant. Problems with my wife? "I'll deal with them tomorrow." Kids acting up? "I'll deal with them tomorrow." But the tomorrows were just like the yesterdays. It didn't matter what day it was, all I ever thought about was how to get more drugs. I was like a starving animal, driven by this uncontrollable, sort of primitive instinct and need to feed my hunger for drugs at all costs.

This obsession with alcohol and other drugs can make us feel like we're going crazy. We could compare it to a man who is born with a depth perception problem that prevents him from being able to judge heights or distances correctly, and then this person decides to take up rock climbing just for the thrill of it. No amount of warnings about hurting himself or others can talk him out of his need to climb and feel the rush of excitement it gives him, even though it makes no sense.

Eventually he runs out of luck and is injured. He promises his family he'll stop rock climbing, but a week later he's back at it. This time he falls a hundred feet, hits his head on a rock, and ends up in the hospital with a fractured skull. He promises to stop rock climbing for good. But in a few weeks, after sneaking off to take on the most challenging rock face in the area, he falls again and breaks both of his legs. Now he's desperate. His wife divorces him. He can no longer work. He's constantly teased. He finally checks into the psychiatric ward of a hospital for therapy, hoping to forever erase his obsessive thoughts of rock climbing. On the day he gets out, he drives back to the same site, and he's hardly begun climbing when he falls and breaks his back. Substitute addiction for rock climbing in this story and you've got a picture of what obsessive thinking is like for alcoholics and addicts.

· · ·

Whether or not we have an addiction disorder, any of us can go through periods of faulty thinking where we resist changing our negative behavior by blaming others for our problems. It's only human to play the "if only" game at such times as a way to avoid taking responsibility for our own lives and actions: "If only my boss weren't so unfair, I'd be more successful" or "If only I were better looking, I'd get more dates."

For those of us with addiction, "if only" thinking is an

especially useful way to excuse our behavior: "If only my parents weren't abusive, I wouldn't have to use heroin to escape my pain," "If only I weren't so shy (or anxious or depressed), I wouldn't need to drink to feel comfortable," or "If only I weren't so fat, I wouldn't have to take speed to keep my weight down." It's easy to fall into this type of addictive thinking because it's often filled with half-truths. Our parents may have been abusive. We might really be shy, anxious, or depressed. We might be overweight. But those things are only part of the picture. Millions of other people face these issues, and they don't have problems with alcohol or other drugs. What makes us different is that we have a disease that is, as the AA Big Book says, "cunning, baffling, powerful!"[1] It can hijack our brains and at the same time convince us we're actually still in charge.

As our disease progresses, we tend to become the center of our own universe. Everyone else's needs shrink in importance compared to our enormous need for the next drink, the next fix. We often attempt to appear special and try to convince ourselves and others that we "deserve" special treatment. We believe we're different when it comes to how alcohol and other drugs affect us—that we can "hold our liquor" more than others or are able to do our jobs even better

1. *Alcoholics Anonymous,* 4th ed. (New York: Alcoholics Anonymous World Services, 2001), 58–59.

when high on cocaine or marijuana. This sort of thinking is called "grandiosity." However, the crazy thing about addiction is that, while we may fool ourselves about how very important we are, grandiosity is really a cover for our deep feelings of shame and low self-worth. These feelings only increase with our out-of-control drinking and using. We feel large and small at the same time—we are Dr. Jekyll and Mr. Hyde all over again. Here is how Rolf experienced grandiosity.

> I used to run with this bad-ass biker gang in California in the early 1980s, back when meth was first coming into this country. In fact, we used to smuggle it in from Mexico in the crankshafts of our motorcycles— which is why meth is called crank. I'm ashamed of that now, but back then all I cared about was hanging out, partying, boozing it up, and taking drugs with my gang. We thought we were better than anybody else, that the world should and did revolve around us. I didn't have many clear-headed moments, but when I did have one, I hated myself and who I had become: a loud-mouthed alcoholic and drug addict who made money off the misery of others. I hit rock bottom and finally admitted that I could no longer control my use. It took several times in rehab and trying out many recovery groups, but I

actually found a sober biker group. We pray and play together, and our motto is "Spread the message—not the disease." With their help and the help of my higher power, I found that life doesn't end when you give up drinking and drugging like I thought it would. It begins. That's what I call a miracle.

Some of us use our grandiosity and other addictive thinking to justify criminal behavior, whether it's stealing drugs or money, or prostituting ourselves to buy drugs, or driving while we're drunk or high. At the extreme, some of us develop criminal thinking patterns where we excuse our crimes to ourselves or others. We might do things like blame other people, especially the police or other authorities; see ourselves as better, smarter, or more important than others; see ourselves as victims; or use our physical power or our words when faced with other people's opinions or objections. This is especially dangerous if we end up in prison, where, unless there's a good alcohol and drug treatment program or AA or NA, we're likely to just learn to be better criminals. In this case, we'll use again the first chance we get. If we're used to hanging out with people who break the law and use drugs all the time, then we're living in a culture where our identity is defined by drugs. It's easy to go back to that environment that got us locked up in the first place. And yet, even if we do end up in prison, there are thousands of men and women who succeed after prison. They come out ready, willing, and able to change their thinking and their lives. By working with a parole officer or social service agency, going to AA or NA meetings, getting job training, and, when possible, finding ways to form healthy relationships with their family members, many people have truly started over and replaced a criminal lifestyle with a recovery lifestyle.

. . .

Whether it's criminal thinking or our everyday mind tricks, the mixed-up thoughts that come with an addiction disorder might be caused by more than us just wanting to fool ourselves. Brain chemistry imbalances or trauma (or both) can also cause distorted thinking and emotions. And we have to deal with these things along with our addiction. Sharma is an army veteran who came back from the war in Iraq totally messed up.

> I saw and experienced terrible things in Iraq. I saw little kids get killed, and I just barely escaped getting raped by an officer. I felt like a stranger when I came home after my tour. I couldn't relate to anybody. My drinking and drugging got so bad that one night I loaded my pistol, got in my car, and started driving as fast as I could. The cops started chasing me, and when they finally pulled me over and told me to get

out of my car, I grabbed my gun, and we had this standoff. I wanted them to kill me—I found out later they call this "police-assisted suicide." Luckily, the female officer was able to get through to me, and I dropped my weapon. I've been in therapy since then and belong to a women's recovery group. It's taken some time, but day by day, with the help of meetings, meditation, and medication, I'm getting my life back.

Like Sharma, many people who abuse or become addicted to alcohol and other drugs also have other brain disorders. These may include bipolar disorder, depression, anxiety disorders, or in her case, post-traumatic stress disorder (PTSD). Some people are born with or develop these brain disorders later in life. Others, like Sharma, might get them from a trauma they experienced. Often people who have these disorders turn to alcohol and other drugs to "medicate" or numb their mental pain, and this abuse can lead to addictive use. On the other hand, alcohol or other drug addiction can cause a mental disorder. And sometimes an addiction disorder and a mental disorder happen at the same time, and neither caused the other. However they occur, these are called *co-occurring* or *dual disorders.*

The good news is that co-occurring disorders can be treated successfully at the same time. For some mental health disorders, medications such as antidepressants are needed. These aren't addictive chemicals and so professionals, as well as AA and NA, accept that we can take them and still be considered clean and sober (abstinent). It is important for those of us with co-occurring disorders to understand that just because we treat one problem, it doesn't mean the other one will magically just "go away" too. Stopping drinking or drugging will not cure our mental disorder any more than treating our mental disorder will cure our addiction disorder. Taking medication and being treated for depression or some other mental disorder doesn't mean we can now safely drink or take addictive drugs. Most often, mixing the medications used for mental health disorders with alcohol and other drugs make the medications less effective and can actually be dangerous. Recovery from an addictive disorder—whether it's co-occurring or not—requires ongoing abstinence. If we're taking medication, we also continue to work our recovery program and seek counseling for our mental health disorder as well.

Sometimes people with co-occurring mental health and addiction disorders don't feel that their needs are met in traditional AA or NA groups. This might be because another member has an outdated attitude about medications, thinking that using any type of drug is bad ("A drug is a drug is a drug"); or because they don't feel free to talk about their mental illness as well as their addiction in the group. Today, there are Twelve Step groups that are designed specifically for people with co-occurring disorders. These include Dual Recovery Anonymous (DRA), Dual Diagnosis Anonymous (DDA), and Double Trouble in Recovery (DTR). At these group meetings, people talk about recovering from both addiction disorders and mental disorders.

Medical and mental health experts now understand that recovery can mean different things to different people in different situations. In the world of medicine, recovery usually means a cure. If you break your leg, you are recovered when the bone has healed, you are walking again, and you gain your full strength. With addiction, recovery begins with abstinence—when we've stopped using any mood-altering chemicals. But just not using doesn't mean we're cured. That's because addiction is a chronic, lifelong illness of the mind, body, and spirit that requires us to work on repairing the damage to all three dimensions of our lives. Recovery from addiction is a healing journey that we take each day for the rest of our lives.

Whether we just have an addiction to alcohol or other drugs, or we also have a co-occurring mental disorder, our world gets smaller as our disorders get larger because of our addictive thinking, our obsession with alcohol and other drugs, our shame, and our secrecy. The stigma (the shame) that surrounds addiction and mental illness can cut us off from people and make us feel lonely. It's painful to be unfairly judged by people who don't yet know that addiction and mental health disorders are both treatable biological diseases—not personal or moral weaknesses.

. . .

The best solution for loneliness is to reach out for help. If we have found that we haven't been able to beat our addiction on our own, even with our best thinking and efforts, we may discover that the solution is to depend on something greater than ourselves for help. This is an important step on the way to recovery. In the next chapter, we'll explore how we can experience that "power greater than self," or "higher power" in many ways—through professional help, our recovery group, our Twelve Step program, our family and friends, and, for many of us, through the God of our understanding.

4

Addiction Is a Disorder of the Spirit

We've talked about how addiction takes a toll on our bodies and why some addiction professionals call it a "brain disease." We've also learned how alcohol and other drugs affect our minds by twisting our thinking and beliefs, and how we can harm ourselves and others when we base our actions on such faulty thinking. But what does it mean when we say that addiction is a disorder of the spirit?

Addiction is a kind of "soul sickness" that infects our very character—that part of us that shows up in our conscience (sense of right and wrong), our morals or principles, our ability to connect with other people in real and deep ways, and in the way we think about religion or God or spirituality. The more serious our alcohol and drug use gets, the more wounded our spirits become. We become less dependable because of our addictive behaviors and notice that others are beginning to distrust us. As they lose faith in us, we also lose faith in ourselves. We might come to think of ourselves as weak, even bad, people. To get better, we'll need to learn the hard lesson that we aren't bad people trying to become good, but sick people trying to get well.

The challenge is that as our need for mood-altering chemicals increases, our addictive thinking puts drinking and using first. At this point, alcohol and drugs may become more important than our morals and values—no matter how deeply we may believe in them. We often begin to isolate or cut ourselves off from others as the responsibility we feel to our families and our desire to do the things we used to love decreases. Our relationships with our loved ones suffer, and we become disconnected from them and from our true selves.

A number of us begin doing illegal and dangerous things that can land us in jail or prison and further separate us from society. For example, we might get in trouble for driving under the influence of alcohol or drugs, or get arrested for drug dealing, prostitution, stealing, domestic abuse, and other violent acts. When things get this bad because of our alcohol and other drug use, we can either become even more distant from ourselves and others, or we can finally realize how unmanageable our lives have become. Some of us see such times as a wakeup call to put our lives back in order and stop using mood-altering chemicals. Most alcoholics and addicts who enter recovery experience a low point—

often called "hitting bottom," or just getting "sick and tired of being sick and tired"—before we become ready to accept help and rejoin the human race.

In recovery, we work to repair those connections that make us fully human. This is what we mean by "spirit": It's the thread that connects us to the world. It's a larger force that links us to our loved ones, our community, to nature, or to our understanding of God—to some power that is beyond ourselves. To begin healing from this disorder of the spirit, we need to face the fact that our best efforts to control our use or quit using by ourselves have ended in failure. We are *powerless* over alcohol and other drugs. As the NA text puts it, "It took a while for some of us to realize that our lives had become unmanageable. For others, the unmanageability of their lives was the only thing that was clear. We knew in our hearts that drugs had the power to change us into someone that we didn't want to be."[1]

Most of us don't like the idea of powerlessness. We like to think we always have choices and have control over our lives. And yet, we all experience powerlessness every day. Unless we know how to seed clouds, we have no power over the weather. And though we can influence other people, we can't really control them. Nor do we have the power to control the

---

1. *Narcotics Anonymous,* 6th ed. (Van Nuys, CA: Narcotics Anonymous World Services, 2008), 22.

health and safety of ourselves and our loved ones—accidents and illnesses often just come out of the blue. In the same way, there are those of us who have no power over alcohol or other drugs.

. . .

While we can't control everything, we do have choices. We can choose to remain indoors in bad weather or to protect ourselves by wearing a raincoat or carrying an umbrella. We can choose how we respond and react to others and if we want to work on shared goals. We can practice preventative health care and go to the doctor when we're injured or have symptoms of an illness. And we can seek help for an addiction disorder. The interesting thing about powerlessness is that once we accept it, we gain a new and more realistic understanding of the personal power that we do have. Our real strength sometimes comes from admitting what we can't control.

Sometimes we're like a child who puts her index fingers into a Chinese finger puzzle. The more she pulls, trying to release her fingers from the webbed tube, the tighter the hold of the tube becomes. Finally, the child discovers that all she has to do is let go and the tube will slacken enough to let her fingers easily slide out. In much the same way, we've struggled and pulled all on our own, trying to break free from

ADDICTION IS A DISORDER OF THE SPIRIT

addiction. We didn't realize that there is a solution to the puzzle and that we can indeed release ourselves from addiction's powerful grip. The first step in solving this puzzle is to let go of the idea that we can control our drinking and other drug use. The second step is accepting that there is a solution to the puzzle but that we can't find the answer on our own. Accepting our powerlessness and realizing there is a power outside ourselves that can help us are important moves, but they will take us only so far. We have to then be willing to "turn ourselves over" to that power, or "surrender." We need to give up on the idea that we can solve our addiction by willpower alone.

But before we're ready to surrender to anything, we want to understand what exactly we're surrendering to. We want to be positive that we really will be in good hands. And the idea of turning to a higher power for help may seem strange to many of us. When we hear the term *higher power* at AA or NA meetings or when we read those words in their materials, we often have questions about what this means. We may be especially confused when we read and hear the word "God" so much in these programs, since we're also told that we can decide for ourselves what our own higher power is. Also, we may have noticed that the AA Big Book and other writings include traditional male-focused and religious language, like discussing God as a "he." We might wonder if we can really choose a God of our own understanding as we've been told or if we need to think of God in this way. It helps to remember that the Big Book was written in 1939, when male-focused language that used Christian terms to describe spiritual ideas was common. The programs of AA and NA have grown and changed as our culture has become more inclusive and accepting of people regardless of their gender, sexual orientation, race, ethnic background, or religion—including those of us who do not practice a religion. Even back in the 1930s, Bill W. understood that many people coming into AA would not be religious. This is why there's a chapter in the Big Book called "We Agnostics," which is written for people who are uncertain about the idea of God or who do not believe in a religious god. Despite the outdated language, what is really being talked about in Twelve Step programs is the freedom that comes when we finally find something more than our own willpower to help us stay off alcohol and other drugs.

Here's how Horace, a Native American member of AA for fifteen years, put it.

> I may have stopped drinking and drugging a time or two or three or four, but "staying stopped" was another story. That only happened when I got out of my own way and moved from the stubbornness of "me, myself, and I" thinking to the power of the big-

ger self I call "Spirit." I felt this surge of relief and hope when I finally felt the truth of that deep in my bones. A light bulb went off in my head, and I realized, "Oh, they're not talking about religion, and 'God' doesn't have to be the God I was taught to fear when I was a child." Recovery isn't about conversion. It's about connection! Whatever connects me to my sobriety can be Spirit, which is how I define my higher power.

Horace was able to rediscover the values and traditions of his Native American culture and weave these into his experience of Spirit as a living force in his daily life. In this way, he could trust a Power greater than self to replace his own willpower.

The NA text, published decades after the Big Book, describes higher power simply as a "Power greater than our addiction." It goes on to say, "Our understanding of a Higher Power is up to us. No one is going to decide for us. We can call it the group, the program, or we can call it God. The only suggested guidelines are that this Power be loving, caring and greater than ourselves."[2] This power may be as basic as a treatment program that we finally find the courage to enter or a counselor whom we trust and can accept help from in

2. *Narcotics Anonymous,* 6th ed. (Van Nuys, CA: Narcotics Anonymous World Services, 2008), 24.

working on a daily program of recovery. For many people, this power includes a Twelve Step or another peer support group that recognizes addiction as a chronic disorder that requires living a life free from mood-altering chemicals.

John, a recovering alcoholic and drug counselor, describes it this way: "I have a minimum standard for a higher power. It has three elements: (1) It's not me. (2) It's more powerful than me. (3) It wants to help me." John reminds us to think of the saying "Keep it simple" when we start to get hung up on words and language. Sometimes we even hide behind words to avoid looking at our own truths. This is how it was for Samantha, a thirty-year-old factory worker who is addicted to both alcohol and cocaine.

> It took me four times in treatment to finally accept the idea of a higher power. I could admit I had a problem with alcohol and other drugs, but as a feminist the idea of turning my life over to a power beyond myself really bothered me because I kept thinking of a "higher power" in male terms. I had spent my entire life being controlled by men. There was no way I was going to buy into a program that told me I had to do that in recovery too. I'd go to meetings prepared to argue, not listen. I'd leave upset, thinking, "I refuse to be under anyone's thumb. I'll show them I have control of my life." I had given

myself the perfect excuse to use again—which is just what I did.

Then I got a sponsor who saw right through me. She said I seemed to be spending a lot of time and energy arguing about what *isn't* instead of looking for what *is.* "No one is telling you what you have to believe or defining your higher power for you," she explained. "Before I got sober, I worshipped booze and drugs, like most addicts do. They became my god, and I was totally under their control. You can guess how well that went." She reminded me that recovery works for those who believe in God and for those who don't believe in God, but it never works for those who think they are God. Then she said, "You don't need to believe in a traditional God, but try to keep your mind open enough to believe in recovery. Listen to what works for others, and think about what feeds you—what gives you strength and comfort and helps keep you sober. My higher power is the energy of this group. I call her Zelda."

The recovery path is wide enough for all of us to walk side by side toward a common purpose: to get free of mood-altering chemicals. Our shared goal is to live fully, honestly, with more hope and joy in a world where alcohol and other drugs do not control our lives. But many of us have found it difficult to accept the recovery language right away. Even if we're desperate for help, we may have doubts about whether the new ideas we find in treatment or Twelve Step programs are for us. It's natural to have problems with the thought of turning our lives over to something we don't understand. This was the case for Eldon.

> When I was in early recovery, I told the group I wasn't sure I needed to be there. But someone who had been in recovery a long time said, "Just bring your body at first; your mind will follow." I'm a scientist and skeptical by nature, but I had experienced the disaster of trusting my addict mind so I took his advice. I acted as if I believed what he was talking about. I acted as if what I was hearing at meetings was true and that what people were saying would help me. In my job, I'm used to a lot of acronyms [initials made up of the first letters of words in a phrase or saying], so it helped me to think of "G.O.D." as an acronym for "Good Orderly Direction" instead of something I could only find in church. My actions based on tried-and-true recovery principles came first, but the understanding came later. I trusted the people in my group and what they had to say. In time, I started to trust myself because what I did in following their advice worked. I stayed off drugs and I got my life back.

Eldon described how he "acted as if" he believed the messages in his recovery group before he really did. "Acting as if" or "Faking it until we make it" are ways to get used to the idea of a higher power. This is similar to using a successful mental health treatment technique called cognitive-behavioral therapy (CBT). In CBT, people are taught how to overcome their twisted thinking and feelings by replacing harmful thoughts with helpful ones and acting on the new thoughts until they experience positive results. For example, someone might learn to get over their fear of flying by challenging thoughts that don't make sense ("There are a lot of plane crashes, and if I take this flight, this plane will surely crash"), and replacing those thoughts with more reasonable thoughts ("More people die walking or driving than die in plane crashes; statistically it's highly unlikely that any given flight will crash"). They then gradually start acting as if their more sensible thoughts were true, and eventually, with each successful outcome, their anxiety lessens ("I've flown on thirteen flights now and nothing bad has happened"). "Acting as if" is also about changing our thinking, but—unlike CBT—we change our behavior first and improved attitudes and feelings of security follow. This is what Eldon did in the earlier example.

"Acting as if" makes a lot of sense in recovery because we have the support and are surrounded by other people who have "been there and done that." In early recovery, we are like a guitar student who is given a new piece of music. The student has heard her teacher play the piece beautifully, she knows how great it is, and she has faith in the teacher's ability to help her make enjoyable music as well. Based on this trust, she practices and practices and, in time, the music flows more naturally. If she makes a mistake, the student begins again and practices some more until she, too, is able to experience the joy of making the piece her own.

Some of us have faith in a treatment or recovery program from the start, and we already know what our higher power is. We may have a religious background and are able to surrender to the God we've worshipped in the past. Perhaps we are lucky enough to find a comfortable recovery group and someone in that group who we trust immediately, and then we are able to turn ourselves over to working a Twelve Step program right away. Or perhaps we've fallen so low that we are ready to turn to anything that promises relief. Then there are others of us who let our perfectionism get in our way. We set such high or unrealistic expectations for what we "should" get from a higher power (such as being miraculously cured from our addiction and feeling better immediately) that we aren't able to see or take advantage of the help and support that is right in front of us. There's a story you may have heard about a guy caught in a flood that explains this.

Very heavy rains fell day after day. The river in front of this man's house rose higher and higher until the authorities finally ordered everyone nearby to evacuate. Neighbor after neighbor packed their belongings and left their homes, but the man refused to go with them. "God will take care of me," he told them confidently when they begged him to leave. "I'll just stay here and pray. I'm sure God will save me." The water rose higher, rushing into the first floor of his house. But the man didn't worry. He just went to his second-story bedroom to pray some more. When people in a boat came by begging him to leave, the stubborn man shouted from his window, "Thank you, but I'm going to stay. God will take care of me." And still the river kept rising, finally forcing the man to seek safety on his rooftop. As he sat on his roof praying, a helicopter flew overhead, dangling a rope ladder for the man to climb. But the stubborn man waved the helicopter away, shouting, "I'll be okay. God will take care of me." The river was more stubborn than the man and it rose high enough to swallow both the house and the man, who still sat praying on his roof. He was a little upset when he got to heaven. "God, I prayed and prayed. Why didn't you save me?" God, looking just a tad angry, answered, "I sent the sheriff, a boat, and a helicopter. What more did you expect?"

. . .

Many of us have found that recovery begins when we become willing to change. We didn't sit around on our rooftops waiting for our higher power to rescue us. Unlike the man in the previous story, we "got into the boat" and took the help that was offered to us. *We* had to show up—some of us by going into an inpatient or outpatient treatment program, others by going to AA, NA, or another Twelve Step peer recovery group. In these settings, we learned from people who have stayed off alcohol and other drugs. We listened to how they did it and then followed their example in working through the Twelve Step program ourselves.

The Twelve Steps developed by the AA founders offer a tried-and-true practical blueprint for recovery that has been used by treatment programs and mutual-help groups all over the world. Following that blueprint so far in this book, we have a clearer idea of the problem: We haven't been able to stop using mood-altering chemicals on our own because we have a chronic disorder. Our lives are unmanageable because of our inability to quit on our own. We're also beginning to see the solution to the problem: We come to believe that somebody or something has the power to help us. We decide to turn ourselves over to that power to find out if we can recover our bodies, minds, and spirits from the disorder of addiction.

We are now ready to explore the next stage laid out in

that blueprint—a program of action that will give us not only the tools to quit drinking and using other drugs, but also the guidance we need to recover our true selves. By finding our own version of the path that millions before us have walked, we can find true self-worth. We can reconnect with our loved ones and communities. If we're religious, we can renew our relationship with the God of our understanding. In the following chapters, we'll explore what an individual program of action designed for your specific needs can look like.

5

Beginning a Program of Recovery

The dictionary defines recovery as a return to a "normal" state from an abnormal state. This definition doesn't really work for those of us who are addicted to alcohol and other drugs, since we can't return to what we've never had. Normal social drinkers don't have to use willpower to stop drinking after a drink or two; they simply quit because they don't want or need more booze, or they don't like how they feel physically or emotionally when they drink too much. Most people can take medications like Vicodin when their doctors prescribe them for their pain, take only the prescribed amount, and stop using the drug when the pain decreases—or if they don't like feeling "drugged." But those of us who have an addiction disorder eventually learn that we can't drink or use drugs like a normal person because we have an abnormal reaction to mood-altering drugs.

Some of us start out drinking or using socially, and at this point alcohol or drugs do not cause problems for us.

Others of us have never picked up a drink or used a drug without intending to get drunk or high—starting with the very first time. "Where have you been all my life?" we may have said to ourselves with the first drink or hit. But eventually, anyone with an addiction disorder experiences the same thing: Our bodies tell us we can never get enough, and our minds tell us we don't have a problem—even as our lives become more and more out of control.

For us, recovery isn't about returning to "normal" or learning to drink or use socially, but it isn't just about quitting either. Real recovery means learning to live more honest, meaningful, and helpful lives one day at a time, without alcohol and other drugs. It might mean that we "recover" the rewarding lives we had before we started drinking and using. Or, if we got involved with mood-altering chemicals when we were young, recovery means starting over and learning to "live life on life's own terms" for the first time.

We get to the door of recovery in different ways, from many paths. The kind of help we need to get there is also different for each of us, depending on our situation and our use. We try to find a program or treatment approach that matches our individual needs as best we can. At the beginning, some of us freely admit we can't control our use and have looked for help on our own. This is usually after we have problems with things like work, family, or the law that become so bad that we turn to a Twelve Step recovery group. Some of us suspect we have a problem so we complete a confidential online questionnaire or get a professional assessment and we find out we're right: We now know we have a problem and we're ready to go to the next stage and ask for help. Others of us end up in a treatment or recovery program because our families or friends or the courts took action to get us there. This was the case for seventeen-year-old Mark.

> I first tasted beer when I was about six and would fetch bottles for my dad and sneak a sip. I never got drunk, but I liked the taste a lot. When I was ten, I tried marijuana with my brother in our secret fort; then I tried whiskey at a friend's house. By seventh grade, I drank beer every weekend. I knew a guy who would buy cases for me, so I'd get friends to each pitch in a dollar. By the time I was twelve, I drank and smoked pot all the time, and missed tons of school. At fourteen, my mom got me into treatment for the first time. But I was doing it for all the wrong reasons— for the school, for my mom, for everyone but me. I began using again when I was seventeen, quit school, and within weeks got three DUIs (violations for underage drinking and driving under the influence). They put me in jail and the court ordered me to go into treatment. But it felt different this time because I

finally admitted to someone else that my life was out of control. It finally sunk in, and I could see the consequences of my actions. I realized I didn't just want to stop using. I wanted to recover.

We might enter treatment without being certain we have an addiction disorder, but we get a better understanding of our alcohol or other drug problems after getting an assessment from an addiction professional. Fortunately, today we have many more options for getting help than alcoholics and drug addicts had when the Big Book first came out and called addiction a disease in the 1930s.

Many of us need to go to a detoxification (detox) center at a hospital or clinic before entering treatment (or in the treatment center, if it's available) because we need to rid our body of alcohol or other drugs in a safe place under medical supervision. Or we might not need to go to a detox center, but still need a safe place and time to go through withdrawal before we can fully concentrate on recovery. Addiction is a chronic, life-threatening disorder that takes a serious toll. Our bodies and minds have become used to the presence of alcohol and other drugs in our systems, so we're bound to have negative reactions—both physically and mentally—when we stop using them. How bad withdrawal might be depends on the drug. The good news is that there are medications and other medical interventions to help us.

The physical and mental symptoms of withdrawal can be tough to go through. At this time, we need to be patient and give our bodies and minds time to calm down. It's also important to remember that the medical and mental health communities have made huge advances in the treatment of addiction disorders. We talked earlier about the medications that are available to help with withdrawal, cravings, and maintaining sobriety. Also, there are mental health and counseling therapies that have been proven to help us rid our bodies and minds of the toxic effects of the drugs that have overtaken our lives. For most of us who have either been through a treatment program or are working a Twelve Step program, part of our physical recovery (along with remaining abstinent from toxic, addictive substances) has meant making dramatic changes in our lifestyle. This can include starting to eat a healthy, balanced diet and getting regular exercise for the first time in years. Also, although it's tempting to tell ourselves that we can't quit everything at once, most of us who are addicted to nicotine actually find it easier to quit smoking cigarettes or chewing tobacco at the same time we quit using alcohol or other drugs. That's because many of the treatment and recovery approaches we use to quit alcohol and drugs work with nicotine too. For so many of us—especially those of us addicted to alcohol—smoking and using went hand in hand. In recovery, we may have found that the ritual of lighting up and smoking a cigarette triggered the urge to drink, so it made sense to quit both alcohol and nicotine at the same time. In order to experience the feeling of well-being that comes with abstinence, we need to take care of our bodies, just as we need to take care of our minds and spirits by working a Twelve Step program.

Treatment is a time for healing that sets the stage for further recovery. Some of us go to an outpatient treatment program weekly or several times a week. This kind of program likely offers addiction education and individual and group therapy sessions. Others of us—especially if we have a more severe addiction or co-occurring disorder problems—might need to stay in a treatment facility for a time because we need additional mental health and medical services, including medications for conditions like anxiety or depression. After such inpatient treatment, we might stay at a halfway house or sober living apartment or residence for a time if these options are available. These places offer us safe and controlled settings that help us slowly reenter the world as people in recovery.

Steps One through Three

Whatever path we take to get there, and whether we go to inpatient or outpatient treatment, the recovery process begins when we get out of our own way and begin to trust that someone or something else can do for us what we couldn't do for ourselves. When we reach this point and agree that we have a disorder of the body, mind, and spirit, as described in chapters 2–4 of this book, we have already taken the first three of the Twelve Steps of recovery set forth in both AA's Big Book and the NA basic texts:

1. We admitted we were powerless over alcohol—that our lives had become unmanageable. (The NA text reads: "We admitted that we were powerless over our addiction, that our lives had become unmanageable.")

2. Came to believe that a Power greater than ourselves could restore us to sanity.

3. Made a decision to turn our will and our lives over to the care of God *as we understood Him.*

In Step One, we acknowledge the problem of addiction: that once we start, we cannot stop using alcohol and other drugs. In Step Two, we become willing to change and believe that there is a solution—a power that can relieve us of the insanity of addiction. In Step Three, we decide to trust in our belief and in the source of help we've chosen (or that was chosen for us). We decide to stop drinking and using, and we begin to recover from our addiction disorder. With this understanding of the problem and the suggested solution, we are ready to take action. As both the Big Book and NA text remind us, all that is required to recover is a spirit of "willingness, honesty and open mindedness."[1]

The AA founders had good reasons for laying out the Twelve Steps in the way they did. The Steps follow a logical progression that takes us from *believing* that recovery is possible to *knowing* it is possible. All inventors, visionary leaders, and scientists follow a similar process: First they believe something is possible, then they decide to act on their beliefs, and finally they take the actions necessary to get the results they believe are possible. People like the Wright brothers, who gave us controlled flight; Martin Luther King Jr., who brought equality and freedom to African Americans; Marie Curie, who gave us the first theory of radioactivity, all went through these steps to achieve their goals. Recovery is just this straightforward: If we follow the suggestions offered in the Twelve Steps in the order they are presented, we can get the results that are promised. We suggest that as we review the individual Steps in this and the next couple of chapters, you stop reading from time to time and go to appendix A in the back of this book and read through all of the Twelve Steps to remind yourself how each Step fits into this logical progression.

---

1. *Alcoholics Anonymous,* 4th ed. (New York: Alcoholics Anonymous World Services, 2001), 568; *Narcotics Anonymous,* 6th ed. (Van Nuys, CA: Narcotics Anonymous World Services, 2008), 96.

Step Four

To move from an idea and belief to action, we need to figure out what gets in the way of reaching our goals. For addicts, many of these stumbling blocks are linked to the wreckage of our past, both from our drinking and using days and from any family and social problems or drawbacks we may have experienced. As we begin to accept help, it's important that we look honestly at who we are and what we've done that still causes us to feel resentful, fearful, and ashamed—anything that might make us want to drink or use again.

In treatment programs, we talk to counselors or other addiction professionals and work in groups with other addicts to uncover and share these feelings. We also look honestly at how our past harmful actions were examples of our character flaws and moral failings. We don't do this to create blame or shame, but to "clean house" so we can tackle the disorder of our spirit and reclaim our sense of worth and belonging. As we uncover these shortcomings, we also can see how they have covered up the real character and moral strengths that give our lives meaning and worth. Just like a real house cleaning, we remove the trash that clutters our minds and spirits and hides the inner beauty and goodness we've forgotten we have.

If we begin recovery in AA or NA, we accomplish this same goal with the Fourth of the Twelve Steps, which reads:

Made a searching and fearless moral inventory of ourselves. This Step is also included in many treatment programs that use the Twelve Steps as a part of their approach. AA's Big Book explains that a "moral inventory" is like a business inventory, where a business owner sorts through products to see which are usable, which are damaged, and which can't be sold. When we take our own personal inventory, we list our character traits, behaviors, and distorted thoughts and feelings that feed our addictive behavior. We also take note of our positive traits and moral principles, which may have been hidden during our active addiction. These are things that can help us in recovery. In addition, we list the people who may have been harmed by our addictive behavior— including ourselves. In active addiction we can flood our minds with resentments, fear, and remorse—thoughts that can keep us miserable and open to drinking and drugging. A business that tries to sell damaged goods goes broke. An addicted person who clings to damaged thoughts and feelings also goes "broke" by getting drunk or high again.

Step Four builds on what we covered in chapter 1 of this book, when we talked about the importance of telling our stories about our alcohol and other drug use. The "searching and moral inventory" we do in Step Four helps us move to the next level. Here we take responsibility for our actions and uncover any shame and guilt we feel because of our past actions. Shame is feeling bad about who we are. Uncovering the source of our shame involves work that we can only do if our minds and hearts are unclouded by mood-altering chemicals. It's work that we'll do over the months and years ahead as we start to experience the rewards of a drug-free life. Guilt is feeling bad about things we've done. It's a healthy emotion that tells us we have moral principles that we haven't been living up to. The moral inventory in Step Four is a practical tool for remembering what we've done to betray our principles and for reminding ourselves why those principles are important to us.

If some of our past harms were illegal acts that haven't been discovered or dealt with, we need to decide who should see our list and if this person is in a position to keep this information confidential. We also have to decide if we're ready to face any legal consequences for our actions, including how these outcomes will affect our loved ones as well as any victims of our crimes. This will become especially important when we do our Fifth Step. Our first order of business is to take responsibility for our feelings and actions so we don't live with the fear, shame, and remorse that will push us to drink and use again.

When we take such an honest look at ourselves, we practice humility—we set our ego (our sense of self) aside, stop pretending, and confront our real selves with courage.

Humility comes when we stop reacting to people defensively out of our shame and guilt and we become willing to take responsibility for both the good and bad that we've done. We reach the point where we are able to listen to our therapist, the people in our Twelve Step meeting, our Twelve Step sponsor, or our loved ones, and hear how they see us and what they need from us. It's been said that being humble means being teachable.

As we do our Fourth Step, we also begin to "thaw out" and feel again. We accept the idea that in order to stay sober and off drugs, we will need to learn to handle all our feelings—both the positive and the uncomfortable ones—in a healthy and confident way without masking them with mood-altering chemicals as we've done in the past. We often will see how faulty, addictive thinking, discussed in chapter 3, has contributed to the feelings and behaviors that got us into trouble. We can now prepare to face the problems we've never dealt with from our families and in our pre-using days, including how mental health disorders may have contributed to our harmful addictive behaviors by distorting our thinking and emotions. This might mean uncovering past traumas, such as sexual, physical, and emotional abuse. These memories can be very uncomfortable and we may need to get professional help in dealing with our painful feelings. If we're in a treatment program, we can find this help there. If we're recovering in a Twelve Step program, we will need to find a counselor who has a good reputation for working with trauma victims.

When we begin to get in touch with our real selves by working Step Four and listing our flaws and strengths, we usually find that we are neither as awful nor as wonderful as our addictive thinking lead us to believe. Jim, an AA old-timer, had this to say about Step Four.

> I hated the thought of a moral inventory because I knew that to be honest, I'd have to list my kids at the top of the list of those I'd harmed. I didn't want to remember the times I was supposed to be baby-sitting when they were just toddlers and my wife was at work. I'd put them in their cribs, turn on the TV, and leave them for an hour or more so I could run to the liquor store or over to a friend's house to get some weed. I'd come home, get wasted, and pass out. Anything could have happened. I didn't want to face the years of neglect or relive the hurt I caused my ex-wife, or remember how guilty I felt when my son developed a drug problem. But doing that first inventory helped pave the way to change and recovery. And living a life in recovery has made it possible to rebuild a relationship with my kids and have great relationships with my grandkids. Whenever I feel

tempted to use again, I take out that very first inventory I did twenty-five years ago and remind myself of the pain and harm addiction can cause. Then I go hug a grandkid, so thankful that I have this second chance.

As Jim found, when we don't come to terms with our character flaws and the harms our drinking and drugging have caused ourselves and others, we risk a relapse and are likely to start drinking or using again.

It often helps to find someone we trust to help us with our personal inventories. This person may be someone who can provide guidance based on his or her therapy or recovery experience in doing a Fourth Step inventory. This also might be the person we end up sharing our completed Fourth Step with when we do Step Five, which we'll talk about in the next chapter. If we're in AA or NA, this may be our sponsor—someone with at least two years of sobriety who guides and supports us in our Twelve Step recovery program. This person should be the same sex as we are if we're straight, or the opposite sex if we are gay or lesbian. If we have a co-occurring addiction and mental health disorder, it's also a good idea to get support from a doctor or counselor who treats both addictions and mental illness, or someone in a Twelve Step group who is doing well in recovery from both disorders. If we are not in AA, NA, or another Twelve Step group, we might want to have a clergyperson or counselor help us with our inventory. Depending on how that goes, we may ask this same person to listen to our Fifth Step when we're ready.

When we do our inventories, we write them out because it's easier to appreciate our strengths and face our shortcomings if we get them out of our heads and onto paper. Sometimes just seeing our truths on paper or on our computer screen puts them into perspective—somehow it makes them seem less threatening and more manageable. Writing them down also allows us to refer back to them in the future, and we can add items that we may have missed at first. As long as we're "fearless and searching," there are many ways to do Step Four. What's important is that we each need to find a way that makes the most sense to us.

Some of us like to use the categories and methods described in our Twelve Step program's basic text. Many treatment programs have Fourth Step workbooks and handouts to guide people through the inventory process. Many of us simply create a "balance sheet" for each person harmed or the drinking and using situations we want to list—with liabilities (character defects) on one side and assets (character strengths) on the other. Others of us might use the major headings recommended in AA's Big Book: resentments, fears, sexual harms, and other harms. We may also add guilt, shame, anger, or other emotions that may be linked to harming ourselves and others. Or our inventory may be as simple as asking ourselves, "When was I dishonest, or selfish, or fearful, or inconsiderate?" and making as complete a list as possible. Some of us go into more detail in our inventories, and we organize our lists in the order things happened; we may include separate categories for childhood, adolescence, and adulthood. However we choose to do our inventories, it's the content not the format that matters—we just need to do what works best for each of us. Also, remember that this isn't a test, and grammar, spelling, and neatness don't matter. An inventory is simply a list of thoughts, feelings, and behaviors that block recovery. We don't analyze or rationalize—we don't waste time trying to figure everything out; we just make the list as honest and thorough as possible.

Some of us may not see the benefit of dragging up past harms. Or, more likely, we simply don't want to review our histories because of how hard it is to face the wreckage of the past. But whether we look at the impact of our drinking and drugging in therapy, in a treatment group, or by beginning the Twelve Step program of action by doing a Fourth Step inventory, it's important and necessary to face our past. We find that we need to take responsibility for our behavior if we want to have a future free of the insanity of addiction. We made the decision in Step Three to turn ourselves over to a higher power, which means we're willing to accept help and commit to a program of recovery. And so we take a leap of faith and, if we have to, we "act as if," take a deep breath, pick up a pen or turn on our computer, and start writing our inventory.

Corrine, a fifty-three-year-old recovering alcoholic, began her inventory, as many of us do, by listing her resentments after thinking about who or what she resented (had hard feelings about), what happened to cause her feelings, and how those feelings affected her. Resentment is unresolved anger that keeps us stuck in pain. Resentments are the opposite of forgiveness, and the AA Big Book calls them "the number one offender." Unresolved resentment threatens our sobriety because we just keep replaying and reliving the event that caused us so much anger and pain. When we hang on to this hurt, we just end up hurting ourselves and others more. This was Corrine's experience.

> It's difficult to be honest about black-hearted feel-
> ings, but boy did I have them about my father-in-
> law. He was so mean to me, and I fell off the wagon
> a couple of times after being around him. For over
> twenty years, he lectured me and criticized me be-
> cause I didn't go to his church, I believed in gay
> rights, I didn't vote the way he did, and on and on
> and on. He even called me an adulteress because I
> had been married before. I held on to my rage and

resentment until he was dead. I stood by his hospital bed with my partner and started to realize this person I hated so much was just a small, weak old man. By clinging to resentment, I gave him way too much power over me. I didn't like who I became when I let those dark thoughts invade my mind, and I regret all the time I wasted being angry. Writing down that resentment in my inventory, then working the other Steps, helped me to let go of it, which gave me more room for love and compassion. It didn't erase his actions—he really did hurt me—but it helped get my anger out and deal with it in a healthy way. I read somewhere that forgiveness is letting go of the idea that you could have had a different past and that resentment is like taking poison and expecting the other person to die. This all makes more sense to me now. I felt poisoned by my own resentment.

As Corrine discovered in doing her inventory, resentment—whether it's the result of justified anger or not—is one emotion that can eat us up and threaten our recovery. When we list the grudges, fears, harms, and other burdens we carry, we begin to see how past experiences and feelings can affect six key areas of our lives:

1. Self-esteem
2. Pride

3. Relationships

4. Finances

5. Emotional security

6. Goals

One approach to doing an inventory is to list the ways each troubling emotion we've identified has affected each of these areas of life.

When we do Step Four, we naturally find that it's easier to shine a light on someone else's flaws but harder to look at our own actions and reactions to see how our addictive behavior may have harmed others. Many of us find it particularly difficult to look at how our sexual behavior may have hurt someone. We have found that it's easier to take responsibility for *our* actions when we list the person or people involved, putting their role in what happened aside, and telling what we did to harm them and honestly looking at our reasons for doing what we did. For example, we may have had an affair with a supervisor at work in order to get a promotion or feed our ego. If we're married, this harms our marriage and hurts our spouse; it's also likely to damage our self-esteem and pride. We could lose our job, which affects our finances, emotional security, and goals. When we do our inventory, we see how this harmful action affected all six areas of our lives that are listed above.

When we review our inventories, we can see our own role in the incidents we've included. This makes it easier to understand how past thoughts and behaviors can control our thoughts and actions today. As one person put it, "If the past controls you, then a higher power can't direct you." In the same way, we also learn how our past strengths and positive actions have built our resiliency—how they've toughened us up so we can deal with those same areas listed earlier. We begin to see how our strengths can help keep us clean and sober in recovery. For Jacob, a young man in a dual disorders recovery group, including his strengths in his personal inventory was an important and necessary part of his recovery. Here's what he had to say.

> As someone with a history of severe depression, it's always easy for me to focus on and obsess about my flaws. That's what I'm used to doing. My counselor urged me to think of strengths in addition to character defects, so I listed things like sense of humor and compassion for others. I still had way more defects than strengths, but it really helped me to see how the strengths I do have can help me in recovery. It was also helpful to see how I wasn't responsible for my drug addiction or my depression—that both are brain disorders that need treatment. I learned that I'm still responsible for my actions but

> not for the disorders that made my life unmanage-
> able. Now I'm taking responsibility for my actions,
> and I'm committing to a recovery program that will
> give me the tools to stay drug free and manage my
> illnesses.

Change can be scary, and recovery is all about change. We are afraid of what our lives will be like without the alcohol or other drugs that have, up until now, been our closest friend and biggest enemy. What will we do without them? What will it be like to face our feelings and be responsible for our actions? While it's natural and even necessary to fear something that presents real danger, other fears can control our thinking and threaten our sobriety. This is why we are directed to list fears in our inventory. When we accept that fear is normal, it is easier to cope with it without turning to alcohol or other drugs. When we face our past and current fears, we realize that very little of what we fear actually happens. It is then easier to let go of the fears that get in the way of our recovery and to make more room for the peace and serenity that recovery can offer.

An important goal of recovery is to replace negative thoughts and destructive behaviors with positive thoughts and helpful behaviors. We also want to sort out what character strengths will help keep us stay clean and sober. When we learn to understand and cope with anger, we become more patient, tolerant, and forgiving. When we let go of groundless fears, we become more courageous and accepting of life. When we own the harm we've done to others, we become more able to make healthy choices, understand others, and eventually forgive ourselves. When we list and appreciate our strengths, we find it easier to view ourselves as loving and worthy human beings.

· · ·

We begin this process when we face our addiction and the harms that we have brought to ourselves and others because of it. These are the things covered in the first five chapters of this book and the first four Steps of the Twelve Step program of recovery. We're now ready to move deeper into the recovery process and begin the program of action, which will be covered in the next two chapters.

6

Taking Action

The main goal of recovery is to learn to live as physically, emotionally, and spiritually healthy people without using alcohol or other drugs. In meeting this goal, we become our real selves so we can develop true connections with others. We began this process by being honest with ourselves about our addictive past. Then we take steps to develop connections with others; this requires that we bring that honesty, that "realness," to our relationships with other people and our higher power.

In the last chapter, we talked about the importance of reviewing our lives and writing down our character flaws, harmful behaviors, and our strengths in order to figure out what can block our recovery and what can help it. Now we take action, face our fears, and present ourselves to the world as we really are. If we're in a treatment program, this happens in our sessions with counselors and in our groups. We've turned our lives and wills over to the recovery process, and we are completely honest with the professionals and other addicts in recovery so they will know all they need to know in order to help and support us.

Step Five

We have come to a turning point where we can begin to release the feelings and behaviors that have kept us prisoners of our addictive minds. Those of us in Twelve Step recovery begin by sharing what we uncovered in our Fourth Step inventory with another person and our higher power. This launches us on the program of action outlined in the Fifth through the Eleventh of the Twelve Steps. Step Five reads: *Admitted to God, to ourselves, and to another human being the exact nature of our wrongs.*

Jasmine, a woman in treatment for meth addiction, found that there is a big difference between writing something down and saying it out loud to someone else.

> I had no problem doing the first two parts of Step Five when I was in treatment. After all, I already admitted my "wrongs" to myself when I took my inventory and wrote things down. And since I believe in a God that listens to my thoughts and prayers, it was pretty easy to share my inventory with God. But that third part—telling someone else about the embarrassing things I did when I was on meth—was another thing

altogether. I was pretty stubborn about doing that part of the Step, but my counselor explained how important it is to admit our mistakes out loud to another person. She said it helps us accept responsibility for what we did to ourselves and to others and helps us see how making mistakes is a normal part of being human. So, after practicing by reading my lists out loud to my higher power, I took the plunge and read my lists to my sponsor—who listened without comment or judgment. She just hugged me afterward and said, "Good for you. It takes a lot of courage to share your inventory. Now you have one more item on your list of assets—courage!" It was a great feeling to tell the truth and realize I could do it without dying of shame or having someone run away in disgust. It's a humbling and wonderful experience. And I can see now how it's a necessary part of staying clean. I'm beginning to see how good people can make bad mistakes yet still be good people.

As Jasmine discovered, owning our mistakes helps us stop denying how our past actions and reactions may have hurt others or ourselves. We also become more accountable for the choices we made and the behavior that resulted.

When we share our experiences with another person, we're able to examine the family issues and emotional pain that may have played a part in our alcohol and drug abuse. Sharing opens the door to dealing with any anger, fear, and shame we may carry about the harm we've brought to other people or about the harms that may have been committed against us. Some of us may have committed or been the victim of violent acts—sexual and otherwise. Healing from and moving past these experiences usually requires individual counseling; this may occur during and well beyond any addiction treatment program. How much or what we share with someone other than our therapist about such incidents is, of course, up to each of us. What is crucial is that we all get the right kind of help we need from the right people or agencies that can provide it. This is a necessary part of our healing. Those of us who have held on to the resentment and fear that trauma causes got used to relying on alcohol and other drugs as a way to medicate and numb those feelings. When the same feelings arise again, that old temptation to use is sometimes too great to resist. It sometimes takes many relapses and additional suffering until we find the courage to face the pain from our past, come to grips with its effects on us, and finally move forward in our recovery.

It is essential that we take all the time we need to decide who can hear our Fourth Step inventory. The person we choose should be a good listener who cares about us and is someone we trust completely to keep our confidences.

When deciding who to choose, it's sometimes helpful to list several people we trust, then cross off the names of those who don't understand addiction or Twelve Step recovery or who aren't good at keeping secrets. As we've mentioned, this could be our addiction counselor, our therapist, our sponsor, a trusted clergyperson, or a friend who can be objective and nonjudgmental. As the Big Book cautions, we should not ask someone who might be hurt or troubled by hearing our story. And, as we noted in the last chapter, if we have committed illegal acts that we haven't taken care of, we need to be careful about deciding who should (or should not) see our lists and who can keep them private. We also need to decide if we're ready to face any possible consequences if we do decide to talk about these crimes.

After we whittle the list down, we can choose one person from it who might be willing and available to listen to our inventory. Then we contact him or her and arrange to get together at a place where we won't be interrupted or overheard. We also make sure we allow enough time to share our inventory. If necessary, we can schedule more meetings to make sure that we can do a thorough job of sharing. We explain to this person that we need to be open, honest, and accountable. This person is not there to give us advice, judge us, or take away our pain. Their only job is to listen as best they can, with an open heart and an open mind. Asking a person to listen to our inventory is an exercise in trust and helps us to see how we can open ourselves to trusting others—and having them accept and trust us—in the future.

Sharing our burdens—the guilt, shame, remorse, and resentment we've carried for so long—is a way to lighten the heavy weight of the secrets that threaten our sanity and sobriety. We don't do this step to please or impress our listener; we do it to heal ourselves. It is a way of saying out loud—to ourselves and the world beyond us—that we are willing, we are ready, to change and be changed. If we're religious, it's also a way to make things right with the God of our understanding and become ready to accept forgiveness.

Completing Steps Four and Five are huge recovery milestones. Honestly facing ourselves as we are and showing our real selves to others for the first time can be emotionally and even physically exhausting. This is why the Big Book suggests that when we've done both of these Steps, we return home and find a quiet place to think about all the work we have done so far. During this quiet time, we review Steps One through Five to see if we've included all we want to include. This is a good time to also focus on our character strengths we too often overlook as we list and own up to our character flaws. For some of us, this is the first time we've felt fully human and accepted our shortcomings without shame and embraced the good in ourselves with humility.

Step Six

As the NA basic text points out, Step Six—*Were entirely ready to have God remove all these defects of character*—is about our willingness to move further beyond self in the direction of spirit. Being "entirely ready" to let go of troubling character traits and behaviors may sound easy, but many of us have grown so used to our addictive ways that we aren't sure if we really want to give *all* of them up. There's still work to do to recover from the "disorder of the mind" we talked about in chapter 3, even after the physical disorder of the body has begun to heal with time. Listing our faults and past harms and telling them to another person doesn't mean our addictive thinking automatically goes away. Our cleverness in keeping secrets, our defensiveness, our "self-righteous" anger and ability to turn arguments on their heads in order to excuse our behavior, our dark (and often hurtful) humor, or even our self-hatred can still prevent us from taking responsibility for our actions and feelings. When this happens, we can remain isolated and cut off from family, community, and, for those of us who are religious, from the God of our understanding. When we cling to our faults, we continue to suffer from addiction's disorder of the spirit.

Many of us have wondered who we will become or how we will manage without these traits. After all, we have worn them like a bulletproof vest that we thought could protect us from the guilt or sadness we've felt about what our drinking or drugging has cost us and others. We might worry, as Robert did, about what will happen if we take responsibility for the harm our past actions have caused.

> I did some pretty horrible things when I was using and dealing drugs. Many of them were illegal and violent. Five years ago, three of us broke into this fancy house because we thought the owners were gone and we intended to steal whatever we thought we could sell or trade for drugs. But it turns out the owners had a visitor who was staying there. She was an old woman who heard the noise and came into the living room to see who was there. We panicked, and one of the guys knocked her down and grabbed her stuff and we got away. Doing Step Six meant that I was getting ready to accept responsibility for that crime and the other things I've done—but my guilt was eating me up over this one. I could put this down in my inventory and even tell my sponsor in my Fifth Step, but even though I had faced the consequences for my actions and did some time and the woman was fine, I couldn't seem to let go of the guilt over how we treated that old woman. My sponsor helped me do what I needed to do. My sponsor suggested I see if there's a way to make it up to her

and to the family I robbed, maybe by adding her to my Eighth Step amends list. That took a big load off, and I felt I was ready to release the guilt and move on to Step Seven.

"Courage is fear that has said its prayers" is a saying that fits Robert's situation. As difficult as it was—and is—he faced his fears. Now he's ready to make whatever changes he needs to make and face the consequences of his past behavior. This is how he will be able have the character defects that this act represented removed so he can move on with his recovery.

Feelings of fear are normal in early recovery, as are feelings of grief and loss. When we enter recovery, we are giving up something that we have centered our lives around for a very long time. We might mourn the loss of a lifestyle that was filled with danger and excitement—even when such danger could injure or even kill us or others. We might miss the rituals that came with our drinking and drug use—the steps it took to mix a drink; the act of rolling a joint or filling a syringe or tying off an arm. We might feel sad that we'll have to let go of some of the people with whom we used to get drunk or high. We might even miss the attention our negative or inappropriate behavior brought us.

A big part of recovery is learning to identify our emotions

and to give ourselves permission to feel them when they arise. We begin to trust that as we grow stronger in recovery, we will get better at coping with and accepting our feelings as a normal part of life. Until then, we can practice feeling difficult emotions like grief and accepting them without trying to fight them or fix them. We can talk about our feelings with our therapist, our sponsor, or in our recovery group, or write about them in a journal. In time, we can come to experience these emotions as a normal part of being human. We learn that they will not last forever and that gifts like joy and serenity are within our reach as we go forward in recovery.

Step Seven

This is a good time to review our inventories and imagine letting go of all of our shortcomings—the little and the big ways we were selfish, thoughtless, dishonest, or hurtful. When we give ourselves permission to grow and change in positive and healthy ways, we realize we are so much more than our addictions. We discover that the past does not have the hold on us we feared. It does not define who we are now, nor who we are becoming. As the NA text tells us, "We begin to feel better, as willingness grows into hope. Perhaps for the first time, we see a vision of our new life. With this in sight, we put our willingness into action by moving on to Step Seven."[1]

---

1. *Narcotics Anonymous*, 6th ed. (Van Nuys, CA: Narcotics Anonymous World Services, 2008), 35.

In Step Seven, we *Humbly asked Him to remove our short-comings.* If we identify God as our higher power, we might interpret the "Him" in Step Seven to mean the God of our understanding. In this case, we do this Step through prayer, asking God to remove the things that get in the way of our recovery. If we have some other concept of a higher power, we might choose to meditate on those characteristics we struggle with, such as

- lack of acceptance
- lack of willingness
- control
- irrational fear
- shame
- intolerance
- self-centeredness
- resentment
- greed
- selfishness
- jealousy
- dishonesty
- self-pity
- out-of-control anger

As part of our meditation, we might ask our higher power—that power greater than self, however we've defined it—for guidance in letting go of those things that block our recovery. Often that guidance might come through a therapist we consult to help us deal with issues like out-of-control anger. One idea is to write down each of the characteristics we want to let go of on separate pieces of paper and put them in what some recovering people have named their "God box." This is a symbolic way to let go of our shortcomings. Or we might visit a special natural setting where we feel part of something larger than ourselves. We could think about our defects in this quiet place and release these thoughts to nature or the universe—however we might think of our higher power.

When our character defects become less powerful, qualities like love, honesty, courage, compassion, unselfishness, acceptance, and confidence appear to take their place. Here again, we need to become willing to make positive and lasting changes. Step Seven also focuses on humility, which we're learning to distinguish from humiliation or weakness. We experience humility now as setting our egos and defensiveness aside. When we do this, it's easier to learn from our mistakes, our successes, and from what others have to share and teach us.

Step Eight

When we let go of our shortcomings, we discover that we are capable of treating others with the kindness, respect, and love they deserve. We are also able to accept such treatment from others. We can show that we are ready to do this by working to clean up the wreckage of our past relationships and to do what we can to make up for the harms we caused others when we were drinking and using.

We begin this "cleanup process" with Step Eight: *Made a list of all persons we had harmed, and became willing to make amends to them all.*

We already have all the information we need to do this. We just need to take a closer look at our personal stories and at our inventories, and then we write down the names of everyone we've harmed, living and dead. In NA, they describe harms as both mental and physical—damage caused by something we said, did, or left undone. Harm can result from words or actions, whether or not we intended to hurt someone with them. Our list might include family members, friends, acquaintances, teachers, landlords, employers and coworkers, creditors or others with whom we've done business, and even total strangers. Some of us have found it helpful to include ourselves on our lists as well.

There is something powerful about putting these names

down in writing because once we see them on paper, they and the harm we've caused become more real to us. This helps us move beyond any denial we might be holding on to. And when something seems more real, it can also seem less threatening, like something we can actually *do* something about. We get ready to take responsibility for our actions—which is what making amends, or repairs, is all about.

In Step Eight, we make a list and then become *willing* to make amends. We try not to get ahead of ourselves by worrying too much about actually making amends yet. Such worry can prevent us from being thorough and honest in our list making and weaken our willingness to actually make the amends. Some of us have removed that worry by doing Step Eight as the NA basic text suggests—as if there were no Ninth Step.

There are a number of ways to do this Step. We can include the reasons for making amends next to each person's name. It might also be helpful to put the names on our lists into three categories of when we'll be able to make the amends: (1) now, for people we can get in touch with right away, (2) later, for people we can't reach right away because we need more time to find them, and (3) never, for people who are deceased, unavailable, or whom we would harm more by making the amends than by not making them. As with all of our recovery work, we can always ask for help from our counselor, spiritual guide, sponsor, or another person in recovery if we have trouble with this Step.

Step Nine

With our list in hand, we are ready to do Step Nine, where we: *Made direct amends to such people wherever possible, except when to do so would injure them or others.*

Making amends is a way to reset our moral compass by truly taking responsibility for our emotions and actions. We heal our disorder of the spirit by reconnecting with others and returning to our community. This process calls for taking a close look at ourselves, taking responsibility, and taking action. Making amends is about how we act, not how the other person reacts. We can never be sure how someone will respond when we make amends for some harm we have caused them. We can only be responsible for the effort—not the outcome. As Chris, an alcoholic in recovery for a year, discovered, making amends is more than a quick "I'm sorry."

> I thought I could whiz right through Step Nine because I didn't think I had hurt anyone that badly. I made my lists as my counselor suggested, and the only names I had in the "never" category were of a grandmother and an old friend of my dad's, both of whom were dead. Otherwise, I intended to make amends to the others right away. The first name on

my list was a longtime friend, and we arranged to meet for coffee. I started telling her how sorry I was for lying on a couple of occasions when I made up stories why I couldn't see her because I really wanted to get loaded with a group of friends she didn't know. I also apologized for missing her mom's funeral because I didn't want to show up drunk. I thought we'd have a quick heart-to-heart, hug, and get on with our friendship. But she really let me have it, telling me how disappointed and hurt she was when I wasn't there for her when her mom died, and how angry she is to know I "chose" partying with other friends over her. She said she needed time to think about all of this. I realized that I needed to slow down and honestly consider how my past behavior may have hurt someone else. My attitude was more "high and mighty" than humble when I began making my amends, and I can see now how that friend did me a favor. I can't presume to know how people feel about me or what I've done, and I can't know ahead of time how they may or may not react to my apology. I needed that "attitude adjustment" before I made more amends. I'm so grateful to her. That experience helped me be more open, honest, and compassionate with the other people on my list. It took her a while, but my first friend called me, and our friendship is back on track. In fact, it's closer and more honest than it ever was before.

The Big Book advises that we should be "sensible, tactful, considerate and humble without being servile [acting like a slave] or scraping" when we make amends.[2] This means that we just do our best to honestly own what we did that may have caused someone harm. We don't argue or try to talk them into seeing our point of view. We are sincere and openhearted and respectful of their feelings, but we need to respect our own feelings too. If the person to whom we are making amends becomes abusive or threatening, we can walk away with our head held high because we know we have done all we could.

We should make amends face to face whenever possible, or in a letter or by phone if the person lives a great distance from us. If the person we hurt is dead or missing, many of us still find it helpful to write an amends letter to him or her and share it with someone we trust, put it in a special place, or symbolically burn it as a way of turning it over to our higher power. Some of us have donated time or money to a cause the deceased person supported as a way to make amends.

---

2. *Alcoholics Anonymous,* 4th ed. (New York: Alcoholics Anonymous World Services, 2001), 83.

Step Nine warns that we should not make amends when doing so risks hurting someone further. This is more common if the amends involved a third person who does not wish to have us talk about what happened. For example, we might have had an affair with a best friend's spouse. We feel guilty about betraying our friend, but this secret has never been revealed and the couple is still together. In this case, making amends might destroy a marriage and break up an otherwise happy family. While making amends might help us with our guilt, we have to be caring and not cause any more harm. Sometimes it is better to say nothing and let our changed behavior serve as proof that we were willing to make amends if it had been possible to do so.

If we aren't sure about whether we should make amends, it can be helpful to seek guidance from our higher power, our counselor, our sponsor, a trusted clergyperson who is familiar with the Twelve Steps, or from our recovery group. We might also need to seek advice from a legal, medical, or financial professional before we make amends for harms we may have caused in those areas.

To be meaningful, our amends should match the harm we caused. If we apologize to a relative for stealing money or not paying a debt but make no plans to pay what we owe, our amends will be incomplete. If we apologize to our children for losing our temper or being overly critical, then turn around and yell and scold them the next day, our amends are empty.

When we make amends to our loved ones, friends, acquaintances, creditors, or employers, we are also making amends to ourselves. By releasing ourselves from the hold these past harms have on us, we are giving ourselves permission to start over and enjoy the love and respect of our fellow humans.

Making amends teaches us about forgiveness. Being forgiven and forgiving others reduces the guilt and resentment we may carry because of what we've done or what has been done to us. We learn that forgiveness does not mean we forget or deny the effects of whatever harm or hurt has occurred; and it is not pardoning or excusing. Real forgiveness changes us inside and can happen with or without anyone else knowing about it.

The Big Book says that if we practice our recovery every day, certain things are possible. People in AA call these the "Promises." These are not literal promises or guarantees for everyone, but these are results that a lot of people in AA and NA experience when they practice their Twelve Step program. They also serve as a handy checklist to chart our progress and show us where we might still be struggling; this helps us identify changes we still need to make. We find that if we've put the first Nine Steps into practice in the order in which they were written, we will experience most or all of the following to some degree:

- amazement at our recovery progress
- freedom and happiness
- absence of regrets
- serenity
- our experience will benefit others
- absence of self-pity
- interest in others
- absence of self-seeking, selfish behaviors
- positive attitude
- less fear of people and of economic insecurity
- ability to handle difficulties
- awareness of a higher power in our lives

Step Ten

"Use it or lose it" is an expression we may hear in many areas of life to remind us that if we don't practice or use a skill or a talent, we might lose it. Doctors urge us to use our brains in our older years to lessen the effects of dementia. We are encouraged to exercise our bodies so we don't lose muscle tone. The tenth of the Twelve Steps in recovery—*Continued to take personal inventory and when we were wrong promptly admitted it*—is a reminder that recovery is a daily, lifelong process. We use it each and every day or we risk losing some of the progress we have made. The work we've done in Steps Four through Nine become a way of life with Step Ten. As the Promises become real in different ways for each of us, we no longer see recovery as "work," as something we *have* to do to remain abstinent. Recovery becomes a new way of life where alcohol and other drugs no longer have a place. This new way of life is the best relapse prevention we have going.

As we grow stronger in our recovery, we automatically do daily check-ins. We've learned from doing our personal inventory (Step Four) how to quickly identify if we're being selfish, dishonest, or if we're holding on to resentment or irrational fear. We've learned that feelings are not necessarily facts, and we know from practicing Steps Five through Nine what to do about uncomfortable feelings when they arise. We seek guidance from our higher power, discuss what's going on with someone immediately, and make amends quickly if we have harmed another. We practice these principles daily and get better at quickly settling disagreements, facing our errors, and admitting when we're wrong. As a result, our guilt and fear decrease and our hope and joy increase. We become more trustworthy, and we feel more comfortable trusting others. When disappointment, heartache, and other challenges occur—as they will do—we learn to feel and deal with our emotions without numbing them with alcohol or other drugs. As Willow, a young single mom with two toddlers, discovered, we learn to laugh more and worry less.

> With the help of my higher power and recovery group, I haven't used drugs or alcohol for more than two years. In my using days, I got used to putting my kids in front of the television so I could rest on the couch and nurse a hangover or whatever other effects I had from the night before. TV became a convenient babysitter. Now the TV is hardly on because we're always busy going to a park or museum or playing a board game. The other day, when my daughter said, "You're a fun mom now!" I fought to hold back my tears of gratitude. I have my life back, but what's even better is that my kids have their mom back.

Step Eleven

As we continue to grow in recovery, we continue to grow spiritually. As we learned in chapter 4, our spirit is about the connection we develop with ourselves, our higher power, our close friends and family, our community, and the world beyond. Our spirit is how we know about our values, our priorities, and the way we need to treat others and ourselves. As we become more thoughtful in our decisions and tune in to our feelings more, we find ourselves stopping before we act and paying attention to what's going around us from moment to moment, day to day. Some of us who practice a religion find that our prayers and rituals have become more meaningful as a way to stop and remind ourselves of our reliance on the God of our understanding. Many of us simply take time to center ourselves each morning, opening ourselves to the gifts that are given to us each day. We also find it helpful to take time before we go to sleep to reflect on our day and what we learned from our experiences, and to remember to be grateful for another day free of our addiction.

With Step Ten, we learned that recovery from addiction as a disorder of the body, mind, and spirit is a daily practice. With Step Eleven, we are given another way to make recovery of spirit a daily practice. This is AA's Step Eleven: *Sought through prayer and meditation to improve our conscious contact with God* as we understood Him, *praying only for knowledge of His will for us and the power to carry that out.*

One way to think of this Step is that prayer means talking to our higher power—whatever we identify that as—and meditation means listening for direction from a power greater than us. Many of us don't worry about definitions; instead, we just think of a daily spiritual practice as a means of getting out of our own way and trusting that the right course of action will come to us if we can quiet the constant chatter in our heads.

There are many ways to do this, from practicing formal meditation techniques to beginning our day by reading a page from a daily meditation book. One form of meditation that many have found useful is called "mindfulness meditation." Here where we simply sit or lie down for fifteen or twenty minutes once or twice a day with our spines comfortably straight and watch our breathing, letting our thoughts flow through our minds without comment. It's good to practice mindfulness meditation in a quiet place, free of outside distractions if possible. Others of us, like James, use our journals as a way to get in touch with our higher power, seeking inner guidance by writing down our concerns or recording some insight that has come to us. Here's how James describes this technique.

> I suffer from a bipolar disorder and an addiction disorder, and find it's very important to keep balanced by carving out some quiet time for myself every day. I start my day by reading a passage from a meditation book. And my therapist suggested that I end each day by keeping a gratitude journal because I have a history of depression and it's easy for me to focus on the negative things that happen. My mom used to sing an old song that had a line, "Just count

your blessings instead of sheep, and you'll go to sleep counting your blessings," so I started a "Blessings a Day Journal." Every night I write down gifts that were given to me that day—things like a beautiful sunset, the laughter of children, a creative idea that I had at work, or a good conversation with a friend. And I always list "another day of being clean and sober." After a couple of weeks, I noticed I was looking at things differently—more positively. It's so much easier to let go of things we talk about in recovery that can lead to relapse—things like self-pity, anger, frustration, and fear—when I concentrate on the good things that come my way. Now I know what they mean when they talk in group about having an "attitude of gratitude."

Even those of us who don't usually pray find that the "Serenity Prayer," which is said at recovery meetings around the world, captures what we are striving for in our spiritual life and in our life of recovery. Those twenty-five words express the central problem of addiction and offer the solution: *God, grant me the serenity to accept the things I cannot change, courage to change the things I can, and wisdom to know the difference.* It is a prayer of surrender and letting go, of trust, and of action where we admit we cannot control everything. In saying this prayer, we acknowledge that we do have choices, and we realize that we need guidance from our higher power to help us act wisely and with integrity.

Prayer and meditation are additional ways that we practice humility—ways of acknowledging that we aren't God, that we don't have all the answers, but we believe the answers will come to us if we're open to them. Prayer and meditation won't stop life's challenges from coming, but they give us a way to slow down and recharge our inner batteries so we can gain the clarity and confidence we need to cope with whatever comes our way.

. . .

Before the Twelve Steps were even written, AA's cofounder Bill W. discovered that there was one essential thing that was required for him to stay sober: helping another alcoholic. That's why many recovering people see all the other Steps as preparation for Step Twelve, where we use what we've learned in Steps One through Eleven to live a life of service. We'll explore what this means in the next chapter.

A Life of Service

With the first four Steps in a Twelve Step program of recovery, we go inward by taking an honest look at our addiction and what it has done to our lives and to those around us. Then, as we work through Steps Five through Eleven, we slowly turn *outward*, by moving from ourselves to others and from self to service.

Shirley Chisholm, the first African American woman to serve in the U.S. Congress, described service as "the rent we pay for the privilege of living on this earth." Those of us in recovery might add that service also pays the rent for the privilege of living in the world as grateful recovering addicts and alcoholics, free of our addiction to mood-altering chemicals. By the time we reach Step Twelve, we realize that to maintain or stay in recovery, we can't live in isolation, cut off from the people and things we care about. We have reclaimed our humanity and remembered that to be fully human means to live in community. We have accepted the help that has been given to us, and we have done the hard work of making our recovery program a way of life, one day at a time. We are ready now to give to others what has been given to us.

None of us works a perfect recovery program. Recovery, like life, is often one step forward and two steps back. Most of us will need to return to Step One every now and then to remember that we can't control our drinking and using. Some of us will remember people who we originally forgot to make amends to, and we'll add them to our inventory. Or we might have people we couldn't get in touch with then who are now back in our lives, and we need to make amends to them too. And because we aren't perfect, all of us will have new shortcomings to reflect on and add to our Fourth Step inventory from time to time. We will have days where our old addictive thinking takes over again and we find ourselves on what people in AA call a "dry drunk"—where we create messes like we did when we were drinking or using, only we do this without alcohol or other drugs in the mix. The good news is that we now have a set of principles and practices that can get us back on track. We also should have the support and listening ear of friends and loved ones with whom we have reestablished relationships so we can honestly talk about our fears and frustrations and get back on track. And by now most of us regularly attend Twelve Step meetings, including a home group where we have formed deep connections with the other members who understand what we're going through. In addition, we know we can call our sponsor anytime, day or night, when we need help working a better program of recovery. But one of the most important things we can do to keep our recovery alive is to live a life of service—to help the alcoholic and addict who still suffers, and to be of use to our families, our friends, and our community.

That brings us to Step Twelve:

> *Having had a spiritual awakening as the result of these steps, we tried to carry this message to alcoholics [NA reads "addicts"], and to practice these principles in all our affairs.*

The principles referred to in this step and described throughout this book are the basic universal human values that we uncover and practice as we work the Twelve Steps. These are values we nurture and protect as we continue to live a life of recovery, one day at a time. For some of us, these values are reflected in the religion we practice. Others of us have experienced those values as qualities in nature and human history that have stood the test of time and that we know both with our minds and our hearts to be true. They are universal—bigger than anyone's personal beliefs—and have proven to provide meaning for all people, regardless of background or culture. For example, a traditional Ojibwe

Indian, a Muslim, a Jew, a Christian, an agnostic, and an athe-ist can find common ground by recognizing principles such as honesty and compassion as qualities that bind us together as humans. These principles are spiritual in that they are about our spirit, that connection with something bigger than self that we talked about in chapter 4.

This explains why even people who don't go to Twelve Step meetings or work the Twelve Steps can recover from addiction. They have found other ways to practice these principles that, when made a part of a lifestyle that includes abstinence from mood-altering chemicals, have provided the mental and spiritual well-being necessary for recovery. Here are the essential ingredients that the combination of a Twelve Step recovery program and a Twelve Step peer sup-port group provide: a practical daily program of action; the sense of meaning and purpose that direct knowledge of a power greater than self can bring; and the support of people who understand addiction and the need for abstinence.

If we take a closer look at each of the Twelve Steps, we learn what some of these spiritual principles are and how to practice them:

- In Step One, we learned about the *honesty* it takes to admit our powerlessness over alcohol and other drugs.

- In Step Two, we begin to experience the *hope* that comes when we recognize a power greater than self.

- In Step Three, we find the *faith* we need to surrender to that power.
- In Step Four, we call up the *courage* it takes to honestly look within ourselves and do a personal inventory.
- In Step Five, we learn about *trust* when we admit our shortcomings.
- In Step Six, we learn *willingness* when we let go of those shortcomings.
- In Step Seven, we come to know real *humility*.
- In Step Eight, we realize how it takes *compassion* (a concern for the suffering of others) to make amends.
- In Step Nine, we learn how making amends is an exercise in *justice*.
- In Step Ten, we find out what *perseverance* means as we go forward and "hang in there," determined to stay on course by continuing to take our inventory and promptly admitting when we are wrong.
- In Step Eleven, we discover how it takes *discipline* to establish a regular practice of prayer and meditation.
- In Step Twelve, we discover the meaning of *generosity* when we practice service to others and share our story of recovery.

When we look over the spiritual principles involved as we work each of the Twelve Steps, we see how logically they flow from one to the next. We see how beautifully Step Twelve—where we share our story with others—links back to Step One. In preparation for Step One, we told our story so we could understand the impact alcohol and other drugs had on *our* lives. In Step Twelve, we tell our story so others might understand how alcohol and other drugs are affecting *their* lives. We give of ourselves not to impress others or to get dramatic results. Rather, we give because this is how we will stay clean and sober. We do it as a result of who we've become by working the first eleven Steps ("Having had a spiritual awakening as the result of these steps . . .") and to maintain the spiritual condition necessary for remaining free of our addictions.

As we learn to practice these principles by working the Steps, or through some other equally thoughtful and careful path, our "spirits" awaken—we become a part of something bigger than self. This "spiritual awakening" might be a dramatic "aha moment"—an intense, deep *knowing* that something has shifted; something has changed within us. That's how it was for Bill W. during his last hospitalization for alcoholism when, in absolute despair, he surrendered to a higher power and was filled with the warmth of certainty that he could finally stay sober. But most of us won't have a "white light" experience or one sudden moment of calm certainty. For many of us it was as if we had been in a fog—a long, deep sleep. As we struggled with abstinence, learned about addiction and recovery, and worked (and reworked) each of the Twelve Steps, our spirits slowly came alive. We moved gradually—often reluctantly—down the path of recovery, a Step at a time, until one day we realized that we felt better. Our resentment decreased and we felt more joy. We weren't as obsessed with thoughts of scoring drugs or getting drunk. The Promises talked about in the previous chapter were slowly becoming real in our lives. That's what happened to Cornell.

> For me, my spiritual awakening was a little like how I fell in love with my wife. We were childhood friends and never thought about each other romantically. We hung out in a group of friends and dated other people. We were buddies. She was easy to talk to and we shared the same interests. We'd even give each other dating advice. Then we started going to games and movies together on our own, and one night I realized, "I think I love her," and I worked up the courage to tell her that I did. She looked surprised at first, then laughed and said, "I guess I do too!" We got married that summer. Everything was pretty good for the first five years—happy marriage, two kids, good job—but my drinking and drug use

got totally out of control by year six. I was a mess and I knew I needed help. When I entered recovery, I was at the point of losing my wife and kids and job. I wasn't at all sure about the Twelve Step stuff, but they kept saying, "fake it 'til you make it," so I did that because I had nowhere else to turn. I sort of plodded along, taking their word that things would change if I stopped using, worked the program, let go of trying to control the process, and let things happen the way they were supposed to. It happened little by little, and it happened slowly, but one day my wife surprised me by asking if I'd watch the kids while she went shopping. The year before she had told me she'd never leave me alone with them again because she couldn't trust me—she was afraid I'd get high like I always did. "Are you sure?" I asked her, and she just hugged me, saying, "Yes, Cornell; I'm sure. You haven't missed a meeting; you haven't used in over a year; you got that big promotion at work; you've been great with me and the kids; and things are so good now. I feel like I've got my old friend back." I told my NA group that I feel like spirituality sort of "grew" in me—and one of the other members said, "Yeah, and the seeds of it were planted when you stopped using. You just didn't know it then."

Cornell experienced what happens to many of us in recovery. Our changed lives are proof of our "spiritual awakening." We often have a new sense of direction and calmness. Life still throws us twists and turns and challenges, but we now have the knowledge and skills to deal with them. We have the guidance of our higher power. And when the going gets so tough that we think we might relapse, we also have the support of family, friends, our Twelve Step group and sponsor, our mental health counselor, or a religious leader and congregation who are there to help us stay the course.

Finally, we help ourselves by helping others, and one of the ways we do this is by "carrying the message" to other alcoholics and addicts, which is the second part of Step Twelve. As the NA basic text says, "By this time, most of us realize that the only way that we can keep what was given to us is by sharing this new gift of life with the still-suffering addict. This is our best insurance against relapse. . . ."[1]

When we carry the message as AA and NA urge, we tread lightly, and remember Bill W.'s experience that we talked about in chapter 1. Overeager to "save" other alcoholics, Bill tried to tell them what to do to recover. But he soon discovered that alcoholics (and addicts) in denial are just as bullheaded as he had been when he was deep into addiction.

---

1. *Narcotics Anonymous,* 6th ed. (Van Nuys, CA: Narcotics Anonymous World Services, 2008), 50.

He learned that recovery was not something he could *give* to or force on anyone. But he could share his story if someone wanted to hear it, he could listen to the stories of others with sympathy and without judgment, and he could help people when they asked for help.

Many of us first learned how to carry the message of recovery by going to a Twelve Step meeting and watching others share their experience, strength, and hope. We noticed that they don't jump out of their chairs and "pounce" on newcomers, overwhelming them with literature or information. Instead, they are more likely to welcome new people warmly by inviting them to grab a cup of coffee and have a seat, letting things unfold in their own time. People new to Twelve Step meetings aren't made to feel like they have to talk or share their story before they're ready to do so. After the meeting, a few folks might stay to chat a bit, asking if the newcomers have any questions and inviting them to come back. Many of us left our first meetings curious about how a bunch of drunks and junkies could be so happy, laughing and chatting with such ease and humor about their drinking and using days and talking about how the Twelve Steps worked for them. We often found ourselves wanting a little of that peace and contentment ourselves. Later, we understood that the people in those meetings were actually practicing the Twelfth Step—giving back what had been given to them.

In this way we realized that one of the best ways to carry the message is to live the program, by going to meetings and sharing *our* experience, strength, and hope.

We also carry it by letting those who knew us in our drinking and using days see for themselves how recovery has changed us. If friends ask us for help or information about recovery for themselves or for a family member they think has an addiction problem, we don't diagnose their symptoms or do a street-corner assessment. We listen with an open heart and mind. We offer to share our story if they want to hear it, telling them what it was like for us, what happened to convince us we needed help, and what it's like for us now in recovery. We offer to take them to a Twelve Step meeting if they want to go to one, or we direct them to the appropriate resources so they can find a meeting themselves. We might give them the phone number of a treatment facility or help them find online assessment information for addiction disorders or co-occurring disorders if they have more than one problem. If we don't know what to suggest, we might tell them we will find out and call them as soon as possible. Then we could call our sponsor, our counselor, or another group member for help.

When we attend the same recovery group on a regular basis, we become more comfortable sharing during the meeting and talking to newcomers afterward. We volunteer to clean up, phone new members, or lead meetings. When we've been in recovery for at least a year and feel that we have a solid enough foundation and a good knowledge of the Twelve Steps and Twelve Traditions, we may want to consider being a sponsor ourselves. (We'll talk more about the Twelve Traditions and sponsorship in chapter 11.)

As Rochelle found out, a successful relationship with a sponsor is a wonderful opportunity to practice relationship skills while fine-tuning our own program of recovery.

> My partner and I moved to a rural town of a few thousand people, where there weren't a whole lot of options when it came to recovery groups. But I'm addicted to both alcohol and prescription pain meds, and I knew from experience that I needed to go to meetings to stay sane and sober. So I bit the bullet and went to the one AA meeting in town. That was three years ago, but I still remember it like it was yesterday. As a newcomer and lesbian to boot, I have to admit I was more than a little nervous! After a couple of months, though, I felt more comfortable. You get to know people in a small town and so many of them farmed, like we did, so we actually had a lot in common. I worked up the courage to ask one of the old-timers—a seventy-year-old organic farmer—if he would be my sponsor. He didn't even hesitate, and it's worked out so well. He's like the grandpa I never

had, and he knows the program inside and out as well as all there is to know about organic farming. We became such good friends, and my partner and I love getting together with Hank and his wife to have dinner, play cards, or help each other with chores. Now I've got the chance to put Step Twelve into action even more because at the last meeting one of our new members—a seventeen-year-old guy who is working on an Ag degree—asked if I would sponsor him. (Because Rochelle is a lesbian, she preferred to sponsor and be sponsored by someone of the opposite sex. As discussed previously, heterosexuals should sponsor someone of the same sex.)

We can also carry the message by volunteering to go to jails, schools, or other places that want speakers to talk to groups about addiction disorders and how addiction has affected our lives. We do all these things to stay sober ourselves—not for praise or reward or because we feel obligated to help. We help others because we have learned a new humility and feel deep gratitude that we are alive to share our stories and message of hope. We continue to ask for assistance when we need it, and we receive the help that is offered. Only now we understand that helping others also helps those who give it.

The third part of Step Twelve, *practice these principles*

in all our affairs tells us that recovery is not just about alcoholics and addicts helping other alcoholics and addicts. As Rick, a sixty-one-year-old man who has been in the same AA group for thirty-six years, put it, "Recovery is about learning to become a mirror in all areas of my life—to reflect back on what I've learned from the program. And it's an opportunity to put my spirituality to work." Here's his story.

> I work at a city agency that helps the poor and needy. Neighbors who lived near the agency often blamed it and our clients for any problems in the neighborhood. I knew the clients weren't the cause of the trashy sidewalks or loud late-night behavior the neighbors complained about, but I also knew that arguing with them would only make things worse. Some of us at work got the city to give us trash containers, brooms, rakes, and other tools, and we launched an "adopt the block" campaign to clean up the block. When some of the neighbors and some of our clients saw what was happening, they volunteered to help, and we all decided to have regular cleanup days once a month. I didn't expect everyone to have such a good time working together. When the neighbors saw that the clients weren't troublemakers but were good people in need, they began donating clothes and household items to the agency

so we could distribute them to the individuals and families we served.

. . .

Living a life of recovery makes us more responsible. If we have intact families, we become better sons, daughters, spouses, and parents. If we have jobs, we become better employees and coworkers. We become better citizens, helping out our communities as volunteers, taking part in local politics, or doing some anonymous act of random kindness for a stranger. If we go to Twelve Step meetings, we become more willing to help out, lead, or sponsor. We become better friends and neighbors, maybe getting an elderly shut-in's groceries, babysitting for a relative who's a single mom, or helping clean up a neighborhood like Rick and his coworkers did.

Like Rick, we're learning how our thoughts about others and the actions we take to help them shape our own lives. Words and acts of kindness, generosity, thoughtfulness, and forgiveness often encourage others to be kinder, more generous, more thoughtful, and more forgiving. When we practice the principles set forth in the Twelve Steps, we learn what the AA founders meant when they wrote, "The spiritual life is not a theory. *We have to live it.*"[2]

---

2. *Alcoholics Anonymous,* 4th ed. (New York: Alcoholics Anonymous World Services, 2001), 83.

8

Recovering Relationships

After we've gotten more used to not drinking and using, we realize that our staying and growing in recovery is about more than not drinking or using. This is a time of change where we're taking another look at how we think, act, and feel about almost everything, including our relationships. We are learning to seek out new friends who support our recovery and personal growth. We are also learning how to assess all our relationships—figuring out which people from our past will help in our recovery and which people may threaten it. We are forming new, trusting relationships with others who support us as we learn to live drug and alcohol free. And we are working to repair the close relationships we have with our spouses, partners, and the other special people in our lives.

Recovery is not an exact science, and all of us recover in our own time and in our own way. If we became addicted at an early age and our addiction has lasted for a number of years, we probably have some catching up to do when it comes to our emotional and social skills. But as we get stronger in our recovery, we gain the ability to better manage our relationships in positive and healthy ways. We try out new ideas and ways of being ourselves when we're alone and when we're in the company of others.

When we first reenter the world free of mood-altering chemicals, we may feel a little like strangers in a strange land. But the longer we are in recovery, the more we discover that there are millions of others just like us all over the world. We've already experienced so many changes—inside and out—and we're starting to feel like more genuine human beings. Still there may be times when we seem so different that we get self-conscious, thinking everyone must be watching us, just waiting for us to screw up. We may have served time in jail for drug-related crimes and are nervous about entering society again—feeling like we might as well have the word "criminal" tattooed on our forehead. It can feel like the world has been spinning without us and that the rules about relationships and how to act in public have changed without our even noticing. We stand in line at the grocery store and wonder how all those other people are able to look so *normal.* But we may also notice that the guy ahead of us has an NA medallion on his keychain, or we see a "Honk if you know Bill W." bumper sticker on the car in the next lane on our way home. These reminders that we're not alone help us breathe a little easier. Eventually, we might even meet people in our church, temple, or synagogue who reveal they, too, once struggled with addiction but have stayed clean and sober for years through a combination of professional counseling, renewing their faith, and finding regular support among fellow believers.

As hard as it is to believe some days, we have a lot in common with that guy in the grocery store line and with millions of other strangers in support groups and drug-free communities a state or an ocean away. In recovery we find others who share

- a resolve to abstain from alcohol and other drugs
- an acceptance of addiction as a disorder of the body, mind, and spirit
- a dissatisfaction with the past and a desire to improve our lives
- a sense of needing to make up for lost time
- a newfound hope for the future
- a need for a safe community in which we can sort out confusion and get support
- a need for relationships that will support us on our recovery path

As the saying goes, "there is strength in numbers." Human beings are social creatures by nature. Knowing that we share this journey of recovery with so many others helps us move from "I" to "we"—from the isolation and loneliness of addiction where our main relationship was with our drug of choice, to a realization that we need other people to live a full life. Recovery means moving beyond the unhealthy extremes of our addicted lives to a place of balance where we experience the give-and-take of healthy relationships.

We started the process of sorting and rebuilding relationships when we did our personal inventories, made our amends lists, and then went to work actually making amends. This process helped us tell the difference between relationships that feed our "addicted self" and behaviors and those that will support us as we go forward in recovery. The practice of rebuilding and improving our relationships includes more than making amends to people we have harmed. It takes time and a certain emotional maturity to face our mistakes and take responsibility for how we express our needs and feelings. Some of us will want to bring back the trust we once shared with the important people in our lives. But some of us had few healthy relationships to begin with, especially if we started using when we were young and came out of homes where trust and respect were not common. We will need to seek out our friends and those in our family who do understand and support the changes we're making. We also might need to find new friends who share our interests and values.

Often, a "relationship inventory" is a good way to help us figure out which relationships we want or need to keep and repair. As we learned in Step Four, a complete inventory includes both assets and liabilities—strengths and weaknesses. We can do this inventory by asking specific questions about our significant relationships:

- Does this relationship put my recovery at risk? How?

- Are there still positive things I get from this relationship? Is it safe to stay in the relationship in order to gain those benefits? (Yes or no, and why?)

- Are we respectful of each other (mutual respect) in this relationship?

- How does this person support me in communicating my emotions and needs in ways that strengthen my recovery? How do I support this person's ability to express his or her emotions and needs?

- What interests do I still have in common with this person?

- How do our differences help or hurt me in living a drug-free life style?

As we progress in our recovery, we learn that *the healthiest relationships are those that share a bond of mutual respect, trust, and openness that encourages honesty and acceptance.*

When the Big Book was first published in 1939, it was assumed that most alcoholics and drug addicts were men, and that a "family" consisted of a father, a mother (most likely one who didn't work outside of the home), and their children. As we mentioned earlier, the language in the Big Book reflected the realities and stereotypes of the 1930s, which is why it contains a chapter titled "To the Wives." Although the language may be outdated, much of what the Big Book has to say about marriage rings true for all intimate relationships, whether the couples are straight, gay, married, living together, or dating.

There is bound to be conflict in any close relationship. Before we entered recovery, many of us dealt with such conflicts by fighting and arguing, running away, or trying to escape from them by using alcohol or other drugs. Many of us pretended conflict didn't exist or we used a "Band-Aid approach" to soothe hurt feelings temporarily. As we discovered, however, none of these tactics resolves conflict. In recovery, we learn how important it is to deal with conflict when it arises so it doesn't become an excuse for relapse.

Dealing with conflict doesn't mean we have to figure out who is right and who is wrong. Instead, it means trying to figure out what's really going on so we can work out a better understanding that we both agree on. What are our hurt or angry feelings really about? Sometimes we discover that the conflict really has little to do with the argument of the moment and more to do with feelings about our addiction that haven't been dealt with. For example, most of us feel a sense of grief or sadness at giving up our drug of choice and the feeling of escape it provided, and this can come out as anger if we feel threatened in an argument. Someone close to us might also have been keeping feelings from us that they've had about our addiction. Dehlia found out how conflicts can explode in a relationship when resentments get buried.

> Martin and I hooked up in our early twenties, and we've lived together for five years. Our relationship was pretty intense at first—lots of partying on the weekend with friends, lots of great sex, lots of booze and club drugs like Ecstasy, and sometimes we'd drop LSD. We both had good jobs and a great apartment in the city so we thought we had it made. Martin and most of our friends sort of "grew out" of the club and party scene by the second year we were together. Everyone started taking their work more seriously, and some of them were getting married and talking about starting families, which was the last thing on my mind. Martin worked during the

day and started taking classes three nights a week to get his associate's degree in accounting. I had a job at a hotel restaurant, so my shifts were different every week. He worked and studied; I partied with my work friends, and my drinking and drug use got out of control. I'd come home high and wanting to have sex, and I didn't realize how turned off he was getting. He tried to talk to me about cleaning up my act, and I would for a week or so; then I'd be back at it. After a long time of starting and stopping, then starting again—worse than ever—I had a few blackouts that scared me, and I finally got into treatment. Martin was great—really supportive and I think very relieved that I stopped using and was in recovery. But it was like we were "walking on eggshells" around each other. Then the bickering and all out fighting started. He had been handling everything for so long—house cleaning, bill paying, schedules—and sitting on his feelings that I think all that anger and resentment just blew up. We're in couples therapy now and hoping we can get back on track because we really love each other.

While those close to us may be proud of our recovery, they may become frustrated or even angry about the time lost because of our addiction. This is normal, and we grieve that lost time too. Like Martin in the example, our loved ones may also have built up anger and resentment because they've had to "carry the load" when we were unable to do so. Now is a good time for us to review Steps Four through Ten and make sure we've done a thorough job of facing our past, recognizing our strengths and shortcomings, and making amends for harms we have caused.

Although we can—and often should—seek professional help in repairing our intimate relationships, it is important to remember that *we* can't be the therapists. We can encourage our loved ones to get the help they need, but we can't fix them, change them, or control them any more than they could fix, change, or control us. The most powerful thing we can do is live our recovery everywhere we go, with everyone we interact with, each and every day. When we practice recovery around our loved ones, there will certainly be changes—but we can only be responsible for how *we* handle those changes.

One way we learn to deal with these changes is to practice setting healthy boundaries in all of our relationships—from the most intimate to the most casual. A boundary is an invisible line that separates what we are responsible for from what others are responsible for in a relationship. In the past, many of us have had trouble with boundaries—especially when we were drinking and using. When we have an addictive disorder, we get used to operating at extremes. Often, this meant being too loose with our boundaries. We may have opened ourselves to people we hardly knew, especially if they supported our alcohol or drug use in some way. We may have partied with strangers, or maybe we even sold our bodies as prostitutes in exchange for drugs or the money it took to support our addiction. Or, at the other extreme, we may have set boundaries that were too rigid and built walls to keep out our loved ones who worried about us and who tried to interfere with our alcohol and other drug use. As we stay sober longer, we are learning that healthy boundaries protect us, increase our self-esteem, and also show respect for others.

When we practice healthy boundary setting, we learn there are times we like to be close, and there are times we need to be alone. We also learn that we have the right to say no if we feel our rights or space are invaded. Many of us who experienced some sort of abuse in the past know what it means to lose our rights to an abuser. As a result, we might be afraid to enter into an intimate relationship now. That abuse may have been emotional (where we were made to feel worthless, guilty, or afraid), physical (where we were hit, shoved, held down, or locked up; or deprived of food or shelter), or sexual (where we were forced to have sex we didn't agree to, that harmed us, or that went against our values).

If we, like so many others (especially women), were abused at some point in our lives, it is important to talk with our therapist, clergyperson, or a trusted friend or relative about how this affects us now. If we are still being abused either physically or sexually, we need to get away from the abuser as soon as possible and call the police if necessary. If they won't provide us with safety, there are safe houses in many communities where we can find shelter and protection. Many of us have had to deal with the abuse (and the abuser) by standing our ground and not taking any further abuse, which may mean leaving the relationship. If the abuser is willing to get help, we encourage that, but we don't return to the relationship until we are sure of our safety.

If we were the abuser—especially if we have physically or sexually abused our spouses or partners—we need to get marriage, family, or individual counseling and find better ways to handle our anger and aggression. We may need special, long-term counseling if we have a history of abusing people sexually so that we can learn to deal with any violent behavior and sexual urges in a productive and healthy way. If we have a problem with sex addiction or compulsions (loss of control over how much sex we have or being obsessed with thoughts of sex or with porn, and so on), we will also need professional help, which may include entering a treatment program especially for sex addicts, as well as finding a therapy, Twelve Step, or other support group for working through our compulsions over time.

Healthy boundaries can also protect our commitment to staying clean and sober. Some loved ones who drink or use other drugs to excess may be particularly threatened by our sobriety. They may even try to get us to fail in our recovery by pressuring us to drink or use. They may think that if they can convince us we don't have a problem, they might be able to excuse their own behavior.

If our significant other or someone in our household drinks socially, we can set boundaries around this to protect ourselves. For example, we can work out a way for them not to drink in situations where we risk relapse, including setting rules about having alcohol in the house. If they are using illegal drugs, we can ask them to stop. If they can't or won't stop, we consider the risks of staying in the relationship, especially if they might also be alcoholics or addicts. If loved ones are abusing alcohol or other drugs, we can encourage them to get help, but we don't try to fix them—we use what we learned in Step Twelve and talk about our own recovery. If they do seek help and get into a treatment program, we take part in the family sessions and support their recovery. We can also invite our loved ones to recovery and other social events without alcohol and other drugs. Often, they acted as our caretaker during our using years and may have felt rewarded by being the strong person, so they find it hard to change roles when we get better. We can encourage them to explore recovery groups for partners of addicts, such as Al-Anon, Nar-Anon, or Co-dependency Anonymous. Doing so may help them learn about Twelve Step recovery and deal with these difficulties.

As difficult as it may be, sometimes we need to leave the relationship—either through a short-term separation or permanently—if a loved one refuses to get help and their addiction or other harmful behavior threatens our own recovery.

Our loved ones may have waited many years for us to quit drinking or using, but they may not understand that abstinence is only the beginning of our new life in recovery. They might be suspicious, resentful, or jealous about the time we need to devote to therapy or recovery meetings or recovery-related activities. If we have started practicing a spiritual program or have become involved with a religion as a part of our recovery, our loved ones may be uncomfortable with these changes—especially if it's something they don't understand or believe. Here again, open and honest communication is a key to understanding. This includes trying to understand the other person's position by looking at a situation from their side. We can help them understand why recovery is so important to us by inviting their questions, offering to provide information, and encouraging them to get whatever support they might need for themselves. Binh, a twenty-seven-year-old Southeast Asian man, had this experience.

> My wife was very nervous when I started going to NA meetings after outpatient treatment for my drug addiction. We are Buddhists, and she worried I was joining some crazy cult that would take me away from my practice and from her. She wanted to know who was at the meetings and what went on there, and she got very threatened when I tried to explain the idea of anonymity and confidentiality of meetings. My sponsor's wife was in Nar-Anon, and they offered to come talk to my wife, which worked out great. His wife told mine, "I know just what you mean. I can still remember when Larry joined NA six years ago. I was a nervous wreck every time he went to a meeting. I was so sure he went there just to complain about me to a bunch of strangers. Together, and with the help of Nar-Anon, we learned that it's possible to talk about recovery and the program without talking about the people." I told my wife that meetings help keep me abstinent so I can be more present with her, not less. I explained how the program is actually much like Buddhist teachings in some ways—very spiritual and philosophical and

about living in the moment, taking responsibility for one's own actions, and appreciating the gifts of each and every day. She said, "Oh, when you share these lessons, it reminds me of how much fun it was when I took that American literature class! I loved sharing the ideas and readings with you, and you were so supportive of me going. Maybe NA can be like that for us too—a way for us to grow together. And it keeps you sane!"

We have learned the hard way that trust is one of the first things damaged or destroyed in addiction and one of the toughest things to rebuild in recovery. But we do the hard work, and slowly make progress. By being more responsible, we become more trustworthy in our relationships. We practice being there for others when they need us. We become better listeners and respect and honor confidences—keeping our word when we say we will. Now we call when we're going to be late and follow through on promises, which make us more dependable. Honesty becomes important to us, and we promptly admit when we are wrong. We work at accepting the important people in our lives as they are, rather than trying to control or change them. We practice gratitude and understanding. We try to keep our expectations in check because we're learning that unmet expectations in relationships just lead to disappointment and hard feelings. In short, we build trust by treating others the way we wish to be treated.

Sometimes we, too, have difficulty trusting others because of past hurts. This is normal. As we become more trustworthy ourselves, we begin trusting others more because we have a better understanding of what trust is and how it feels to be trusted. We can practice trusting others by trusting our higher power, our sponsor, counselor, or religious guide, and others in our recovery support groups. Building trust takes time, work, and willingness on everyone's part, but we can't have a real and healthy relationship without it.

Love relationships aren't the only ones that change in recovery. Friendships also go through changes. Many of us have friends who are happy to support our new lives in recovery, so those relationships continue. But other friends—especially those who we drank and used with—might get a little nervous when we stop drinking or using, and those friendships often fall away when we begin recovery. As we inventory or review and redefine our close relationships, we also decide whether we should continue a friendship or let it go. With friends who continue to abuse alcohol and drugs, the decision should be easy: We can't base a relationship on getting high anymore.

All friendships have a lifespan and don't last forever. It's natural for some to fade away by themselves. The things that brought us together—shared interests, children, job, school, or military service—change, and a relationship can lose the importance it once had. How we say good-bye to friends we cannot keep depends on how close we were and the kind of friendship we had. Rosalinda, a forty-year-old recovering alcoholic, chose to end a friendship with a drinking buddy of many years. She sent the friend a letter.

> I've known Lucy since high school. We were cheerleaders together and continued to hang out after graduation from time to time, but it got so we never did anything where alcohol wasn't involved. When I told her I had a drinking problem and was going into treatment, she tried to convince me I wasn't an alcoholic. Then she'd call or text me occasionally from our old hangout to try to get me to join her for a drink. I think part of it was that she didn't want to look at her own drinking habits—but I wasn't out to diagnose or save her. I needed to take care of myself. I wrote her a letter telling her that I needed to focus on my recovery and that it would be best to go our separate ways. I thanked her for being part of my life and wished her well. My counselor helped me with this, having me draft the letter first then share it with her. She said to use short, direct, and nonblaming

> sentences and to circle any "you" statements and see if I could change them to "I" statements. This would help me take responsibility for only my thoughts, feelings, and actions. It's easy for me to act like a teenager around old friends, and writing the letter felt very adult. It was an important step in becoming more emotionally mature. Guess I'm finally growing up!

As was true when we made amends, we can't be sure how or whether a friend will react to our saying good-bye—however we choose to do it. If our plan for ending a friendship doesn't go as we thought it would, it doesn't mean we've failed. It only means that we tried our best for ourselves and for our recovery. We move on.

In the past, our addiction competed with our relationships and probably won most of the contests. Now we're ready to repair the damage addiction caused by becoming friends with ourselves and others in new ways that build trust and confidence and open us up to the possibility of happiness and hope. We become better friends now to the people who stick with us and who we want to be a part of our new lives. We discover new ways to share time with our friends and, just as we're learning to do with ourselves, we can better appreciate our friends for who they are, with all their strengths and shortcomings.

We are finding it easier to befriend ourselves by treating ourselves with the same patience, compassion, and understanding we are trying to show others. We get better at ignoring the negative messages we may still tell ourselves and instead focus on the positive qualities we want to bring to our relationships in recovery.

Practicing relationship skills with people we already know paves the way for new relationships. Recovery sayings like "Easy does it," "Live and let live," and "First things first" have been helpful to many of us when we think about entering new relationships—especially intimate ones. They help us remember to relax and give others some slack instead of getting angry or resentful. Such sayings also remind us that the first and most important thing we always need to tend to is our recovery. We move slowly, especially at first, and try to avoid starting a new intimate relationship until we've been sober for at least a full year. If we're tempted to date someone in our AA, NA, or other recovery group, we resist doing so because we know our emotions are still pretty raw and our judgment may not be the best.

We are fortunate today that more and more people outside of the recovery community understand that addiction is a disease. We will probably find that some of our friends, both old and new, accept and even celebrate our recovery lifestyle. Still, starting new friendships and rebuilding intimate relationships always means being somewhat willing to take risks. At times even when we're doing our best, our interest in another person won't be returned or our expectations won't be met, and we might feel hurt. We keep at it and try again because we have learned that we need to have positive connections with other people to feel good about ourselves—this helps us enjoy life without getting high. We're also learning that we can have fun with others by just being ourselves, because we're starting to like who we are. Dylan, a thirty-two-year-old welder whose social life once revolved around drinking and using drugs, found this out.

> I have way more fun sober than I ever did high. For one thing, when I got wasted on pills and booze, I couldn't remember anything the next day, including whether or not I had a good time. And I always felt horrible in the morning. Now I have a blast at recovery events. Plus, I'm on a softball league, and my girlfriend and I take swing dance lessons with another couple. We've also rediscovered how much fun it is to play cards or board games. Just last weekend, we had a party and played charades, a game I would have been too embarrassed to play before. I can't remember laughing that much or that hard when I was using.

. . .

In recovery, we reach out to others and to our higher power. With this companionship and the recovery principles we are now practicing daily, we get to know others and ourselves better. We form new friendships and tend to old relationships with open hearts and clear minds, using the tools and knowledge we have gained. In a way, every relationship is a new one because *we* are "new" and are living a new kind of life.

Building closer relationships with our spouses and other loved ones and making new friends is an important part of our recovery from our disorder of the spirit. We find a "power greater than self" in the love and trust of relationships where both people are honored and respected. This is truly the gift of spirit. As one person put it, "A healthy relationship is like being shown a piece of God."

9

Recovering Our Families

The world has changed dramatically since the early days of AA and NA. Today's families come in all shapes and sizes, and there is no longer one definition of the word "family." We may have been raised by a mom *and* a dad, a mom *or* a dad, or by two lesbian moms or two gay dads. We may have been adopted or conceived by artificial insemination. One or more grandparents might have raised us, or we might be grandparents who are bringing up our grandchildren. Modern families are sometimes called "blended," with step-parents and step- or half brothers and sisters. Some of us may have spent time living with aunts or uncles or foster parents. Or maybe we had mentors, teachers, a Big Brother or a Big Sister, a scout leader, or people from our church who took us under their wings and treated us like family. Many of us come from homes where our parents divorced, or a parent died or left when we were very young. Perhaps an older sibling raised us, or we were responsible for younger siblings.

Some of us had a parent who was unavailable or abusive in some way. Our parents may have been alcoholics or drug addicts too.

We come from families where either or both parents work, do the housework, or take on most of the parenting duties. Our families still might be "old school" in many ways, including their views of addiction and mental illness. As a result, they might have trouble accepting these disorders as medical conditions. A growing number of us are immigrants. In our cultures, men may take on the traditional family role of breadwinner and head of family, and women are thought of as housekeeper and mom. In many Latin, Asian, and African cultures, addiction and mental health disorders are seen as moral and spiritual defects—not medical conditions that can be treated. As addicts in these families, we often face denial, shame, and even rejection, which make it harder for us to get help and support in recovery. When people from older cultures come to the West, especially to the United States, there is often a clash of values that creates conflict between generations.

The truth is, there is no such thing as a "traditional" family, and no family is—or has ever been—perfect. The happy families we used to see on TV didn't show the different ways that people really lived, even back then. We can waste a lot of time wishing we had a "normal" family, even though we probably don't really know what we mean by that. When we realize that families are made up of imperfect human beings who are related to each other in a lot of different ways, we can let go of unrealistic expectations of what we think our family "should" be (or should have been). This makes it easier to accept our family for what it is so we can get on with the important work of recovery. As we learn from working the Twelve Steps, such acceptance allows us to honestly face what may have been done to us in the past and what we may have done to others because of our addiction disorder.

There are reasons why addiction is called a "family disease." As KimLi (whose story we told in chapter 2) discovered, we might be more likely to become addicted if there's a history of the disease in our family. Our risk for addiction is also greater if we experience traumatic or hurtful events early in life. We are then more likely to develop addictive thinking and become addicted to alcohol or other drugs. But we must remember, our families or past experiences don't *make* us addicts. We are learning that addiction is a brain disorder, and people from all kinds of backgrounds can have it. While our family history and environment play a part in addiction disorders, that's not the whole story. Addiction can happen and cause serious problems even in families that are really healthy.

Regardless of circumstances, addiction is called a family disease because it always affects the whole family—whether or not its members are related by blood or by some other bond. When we are addicted and are still drinking or using, our family members usually adjust by taking on certain survival roles. For example, a nonaddicted spouse or parent might take over running the household, become the family decision maker, or do things to hide or to make up for our addictive behavior. An older child might become the "responsible one," trying to take care of things when an addicted parent is unable to do so. One child might try to be perfect and another might become "invisible." Someone else might act as the family clown, or just act out to get attention or to shift attention away from the real problem—addiction.

When we're in a family system, we're connected like a wind chime. When one of us shifts positions, we bump into another person, who then bumps into another. The result can be a pleasing sound or an unpleasant crash—which is what happens with addiction in a family. The good thing about this is that when we recover, our whole family can benefit too. This can take some time, however, because they probably got pretty used to the roles they played when we were using. And if we've relapsed before, they may be afraid to get their hopes up. They don't want to be disappointed again. Rebuilding trust in a family is one of the biggest challenges in recovery.

Sharing our thoughts and feelings honestly with our family members, and listening to their fears and other feelings without getting defensive or angry, helps rebuild trust. We can encourage them to ask questions about our recovery process and tell them where they can get more information about addiction and recovery (for example, from Al-Anon or Nar-Anon). This can make recovery a little less mysterious for them. And being honest about the things that can cause relapse (our "triggers") can help us put safeguards in place or make it easier for them to support us if we do relapse.

We know that addiction is chronic, or a lifelong illness, and that we will never be able to safely drink or use. Many of us have to learn this the hard way by trying alcohol or drugs again—sometimes multiple times, even after we've had a few years of being clean and sober. We relapse for a lot of reasons, but mostly because we have slacked off from working a daily program of recovery and our disorder of the mind tells us we can use now without the harmful results. Or, we might relapse after going back to the familiar people, places, and things that are connected to our drinking and using. Or maybe we are upset, tired, bored, or going through a difficult time in our lives and don't have a plan for dealing with the situations that trigger the cravings in our addicted brain. Brianna found out she needed such a plan.

> I learned the hard way that abstinence means not using *any* mood-altering drugs. After I had been off cocaine for a year, I thought a little wine couldn't

hurt because I was never addicted to alcohol. But I really liked how that first glass made me feel, and soon I was drinking almost every night. Now I finally get it about triggers and relapse. My group and sponsor were great. Some of them had slipped before—including my sponsor—and they helped me understand that relapsing doesn't mean starting over because I already have tools and support in place. They helped me come up with a plan of what I should do if I relapse: stop using, call my sponsor or counselor immediately, and go to a recovery meeting within twenty-four hours. I called a family meeting and shared my plan with my husband, my sister, and my adult son. We also talked about things that can trigger addiction for me. We agreed that I could call any one of them if I felt shaky about using or if I had relapsed. They said they'd come and get me—no questions asked. I made sure they have the name and number of my sponsor, so they know to call her too. Talking about addiction openly has helped all of us get beyond the fear we had during those first years of recovery. None of us *expects* me to relapse again, but now we all know what to do if it happens. That's helped us all relax and not feel like we're waiting for the worst to happen any minute.

Most of us have experienced how addiction can consume and take over families. Our families probably worried about us. Besides taking on new family roles to cope with our addiction, they may have lied or made excuses about our behavior to others, tried to cure us or control the addiction, or worked hard to pretend it wasn't there. So it only makes sense that when we stop drinking or using, they get a little confused about what to do now that our addiction is no longer taking up so much of their energy. Their behaviors around our addiction may have been unhealthy, but at least they were familiar. Here's how early recovery was for sixteen-year-old Carlos, who was addicted to inhalants and marijuana.

> When I got out of treatment and enrolled in a sober high school, I thought my family would be so happy, and they were at first. But then things got sort of weird. My mom seems so uptight now that she doesn't have to police me every second. And my kid brother went nuts one day, yelling about how I got all the attention when I was using and now get all the attention because I'm clean.

Recovery takes some getting used to for everyone—us, our family, our friends, our coworkers, and others with whom we come in close contact. Many of the things that we are learning about our personal relationships—setting boundaries, taking responsibility for ourselves and not trying to control the other person, listening and not just talking—apply to dealing with our families too. We also need to give our family time to get used to us as individuals in recovery. At first, we'll probably feel stressed with so many new things going on, and so will they.

We might feel ready to go back to the roles we had in the family before we started using. But our family might not be ready for this. Those family members who took over our old roles when we were drinking and using may not want to adjust or give up these roles yet. Whatever roles we take on in the family, it's important to know that we'll make mistakes. And it will take time for others to believe in us again, for trust to form again, and to get past any remaining resentments. It's very easy to get caught up in trying to figure out who or what is responsible for the problems in our family. Our mother might want to blame our father. Our father may want to blame our spouse who left us. Our kids may want to blame us, and we may want to blame ourselves. It's often helpful when our family goes to counseling together so everyone can better understand the wounds that need healing and stop trying to find the bad guy.

Above all, we try to keep the lines of communication open. We tell our families that we know our addiction has been hard on them too, and we encourage them to express themselves. Sharing what we think, feel, and notice as honestly and respectfully as we can helps create new healthy patterns of family behavior. Some of us come from families where feelings were often buried. We may be learning to express our feelings with words for the first time. It will take work to avoid slipping back into old patterns of either shutting down or—at the other extreme—screaming, hitting people, or storming out of the room when we get scared or angry. When we think we might lose control, we might use the Twelve Step recovery tool called HALT. When things or feelings seem to be getting out of hand, we can suggest that everyone take a break and calm down. Then we can find a quiet place and use HALT to check in with ourselves. Are we Hungry, Angry, Lonely, or Tired? Any one of these feelings can lead to the harmful behaviors of our using days.

Instead of just focusing on problems that addiction causes, we try to be grateful for the strengths we get from our families. Many of us come from close-knit families that gave us the traditions and spiritual values that we can build on in recovery and celebrate in our own families. For example, we may have learned the importance of love, self-reliance, and strong spiritual values from our Native American or Latina grandmother. Or maybe we learned about the importance of family loyalty, cultural values, and history from a relative who survived hard times such as wars, economic depression, or traumas like the Holocaust or forced emigration. Many of our parents have taught us the meaning behind family rituals around special times, like holidays and meals. As we learned when we did our personal inventories, taking stock of our assets—the positive things we've gained or have been given—in addition to our liabilities (our weaknesses), helps us keep things more in balance.

Some of us who have kids—especially if our children are young—may not know how much or what to tell them about our addiction or about alcohol and drugs in general. Although it might be uncomfortable, it is important to be honest with our kids about addiction and recovery. What we tell them, and how much we tell them, depends on their age and ability to understand. We can look for opportunities to talk about our addiction, such as when one of our children talks about the drug prevention program at their school or something about addiction comes up in a TV show or movie. Here's Jay's story about how this happened for him and his daughter.

> I was watching a sitcom on TV with my eleven-year-old daughter and one of the main characters came home drunk, slurring his words and acting like a jerk—which was supposed to be funny. I could see her tense up and sort of watch me out of the corner

of her eye, so I turned off the TV and we talked. "Does that remind you of me when I was drinking a lot?" I asked her. She told me it did and then talked about how she sometimes got scared when I'd drink and yell at her mother or her. She said she was still nervous about having friends over because of the times she got embarrassed by the way I acted around them in the past, so we talked about that too. We talked about how addiction is an illness and how I'm working hard to make sure it doesn't "come back" again by going to my meetings and working the Twelve Steps. I told her she could ask me any questions at any time. And I said I'd be glad to do whatever it takes to help her know her that I'm following my program. For example, I would mark my meetings off on the family calendar or read a family meditation with her and her mom at breakfast. Then I asked if she wanted to go to a recovery picnic with me and her mom that our intergroup is putting on, and we're planning to do that. I know it's going to take time to gain her trust again, but I think we made a good start.

Those of us with children try to let them know whenever we can that their reactions to our past addictive behaviors are normal and understandable. These include responses like fear, embarrassment, concern, anger, or even disgust. We try not to overload our children with information, scare them, or "over share" about our addictive past. We wait for the right moment and are honest and loving in what we tell them and how we say it. We can't stop our kids from experimenting with drugs themselves someday, but we can use our stories to help them understand the dangers of drug use and the disease of addiction. And we can create an environment in our homes where alcohol and drug use is not accepted—including use of any illegal drugs, misuse of prescription drugs, or underage drinking.

It's likely that our younger family members will think that recovery means that everything is "cured." Others might not trust the "new" us, or they may still feel the pain our addiction caused the family. Our children may have gotten used to taking care of themselves and may resent it when we discipline them or try to get involved in their lives again. We need to earn back their trust and respect before they're ready to let us return to our role as parents. Often it helps to find ways for our children to "be kids" again—by having a family game or movie night, playing a video game, going miniature golfing together, biking, or doing some other fun activity. We've discovered that the best way to build our children's trust is to simply let them see how we are changing daily in healthy recovery.

Another member of our family may be having problems with alcohol and drugs too. We might want to attend Al-Anon or Nar-Anon meetings ourselves if this happens to someone close to us—our partner, our parents, a sibling, or one of our children, for example. This is R.J.'s story.

> I've been clean and sober for twenty years, one day at a time. I go to my meetings every week, read the literature, meditate, and ask my higher power for guidance. I've sponsored many people through the years. I know this stuff, so when I found out my nineteen-year-old son had a drug and alcohol problem, I felt really stupid—it never entered my mind that he could be using. He knows I'm a recovering alcoholic and that his mother (my ex-wife) is a practicing drug addict. I thought that was enough to keep him straight. But for a long time he just didn't seem to be himself.
>
> Then one day, almost in passing, I said, "You're acting like you're on drugs." He said he was. When I asked what kind, he said he'd tried just about everything. I was stunned—but at least I knew enough not to preach or yell. We just talked. Then I got help from others. When an old friend in recovery suggested I go to Al-Anon or Nar-Anon, I was blown away. I always viewed those as groups for "them" and AA

and NA for "us." My friend went with me to a Nar-Anon meeting, and I confess I was pretty nervous at first, but the familiar Twelve Step meeting structure made it easier. I introduced myself by saying, "I'm an alcoholic and a drug addict—like the people who give *you* reason to be here—but now I need help because my son is an addict too." It broke the ice, and it was a big help to view addiction from "the other side of the fence." It struck a real chord with me when a woman there told me that I've got my story, but my son is still writing his own. I can tell him about my path and show him a path exists, but I can't walk it for him.

As adults, we usually have two families to find our way with in recovery—our family as a partner and parent, and our original family (also called family of origin). When we visit our original family, we recall memories, both happy ones and hurtful ones. Too often, the skills and emotional maturity we've gained and practiced in recovery melt away the minute we enter the door of our parents' homes or get together with other family members. In spite of all the good work we've done in recovery, our parents and siblings or others from our distant past can hook us into acting and reacting like we did when we were kids living in the same household.

We know now that our recovery comes first and that we have a choice about attending family gatherings or visiting family. If we think a reunion or visit might put our recovery at risk, we have the right to say "no." This is especially important if there is active addiction in our family or if a lot drinking takes place at these events. Some of us have found it helpful to make a list of the pros and cons for visiting on a sheet of paper. This helps us see if such a visit is a good idea or if it should be postponed until we feel stronger in recovery. If we decide not to visit, our sponsor or a friend in recovery can help us find the right words to tell them we can't come.

If we do decide to visit family, it's often helpful to think about what we can do to make the visit as stress-free as possible. This might mean staying at a hotel instead of the family home, not staying too long, and, if we haven't already, letting our family know ahead of time that we are in recovery and that we no longer use alcohol or other drugs. We try to keep our expectations—both positive and negative ones—in check to avoid resentment, disappointment, or other emotions that can threaten our recovery.

It's common to put off dealing with difficult personal issues that might cause conflict with the family in which we grew up. Although we've changed, some of our family members haven't, and we may try to avoid facing them. Perhaps we have come out as being gay or transgender since we last saw some family members, and we know they have said mean or hurtful things about gays in the past. We might be dating someone of another race, religion, or ethnicity, and we're not sure if our very conservative family will be accepting of this person. We might have changed our political or social views, and they're now different from our family's views. Some of us feel we need to deal with issues like this now with someone important to us. If so, we calmly let that person know where we stand. But we avoid trying to convince or argue. Instead, we look for areas of understanding and agreement. The AA slogan "Live and let live" is our guide. If a family member can't love us for who we are, we accept it and even part ways if we have to. While we can't afford to let resentments or conflict threaten our sobriety, we still leave the door open for working out our differences. In these stressful situations, it helps to have a support system in place before we visit our family. Simone is a sixty-eight-year-old recovering alcoholic and opioid addict who recently became addicted to her pain medication when she developed chronic back pain. This is how she handles her family visits.

> When I get ready to go home to visit my ninety-year-old mom, my brother, and my sister, I always let my sponsor and my two closest friends know so they can write it on their calendars. Those visits can be

crazy making sometimes, so they know they might be getting a panicky call while I'm gone, and they are also so good about checking in with me by phone or email. It helps to ground me. I also make sure I have the address and times of a nearby AA meeting I can go to. One time, I was even able to do a long-distance phone session with my therapist when things got really stressful. All those safeguards allow me to still have a pretty good visit *and* keep my sobriety.

. . .

Even with all our best efforts and good intentions, some of our families are so destructive and dysfunctional that we know they will never be able to support us *or* our recovery. We may have to face the hard fact that staying healthy and sober means staying away from them. This might be true only for a while, until we are more stable in our recovery. In these cases, we might create a replacement family, surrounding ourselves with people who love and accept us as we are. We discover that we can make new traditions, model healthy behavior for our children, and find the support that was missing in our original family. For many of us, our recovery support group, religious community, or circle of close friends become members of our new family.

It doesn't matter whether we are born into a family or

we create one of our own—if we work a recovery program, we can change our family roles and communication for the better. Just as our addiction damages our family, in recovery our entire family can benefit. For example, we can make our relationships with the most important people in our lives healthier and stronger than they ever were. As in our other relationships and in our peer recovery groups, we can find in family the support we need to live a life of service and meaning that will carry us through many rough waters ahead. With this community of spirit as our foundation, we are able to rebuild other key areas of our life as people in recovery, including our jobs and careers, which we'll explore in the next chapter.

10

Recovering Our Jobs and Careers

Meaningful work is important, whether we're a factory worker, carpenter, salesperson, surgeon, stay-at-home parent, teacher, or a student who hopes to enter the workforce someday. Work makes us feel that we're giving back to the world and to our families—especially if we have children. Having a paying job provides us with food, shelter, and a certain stability that may have been missing during the crazy days when we were drinking and using. While having a job can boost our self-esteem, we don't necessarily need a job to feel that our life is worthwhile. We can find self-worth the rest of our lives by going to recovery meetings, working at our relationships, practicing our religions if we're religious, and volunteering in our community. But if we're not ready to retire and if we are able to work, most of us want to have a career path or a job that brings in some money to pay our way in the world—even if the job is part-time.

For many of us, getting back into the job market or finding

a career means going back to school or getting our GED. Depending on our age, this can be difficult to do, especially if we don't have a steady income. Many states and nonprofits offer employment and education counseling, and we can talk to people in our support network about finding and using these resources.

Most of us know that addiction disorders can affect every part of our lives, including our search for a job, our performance at work or school, our ability to meet employment and career goals, or our ability to even hold down a job. Some of us started drinking or using early in our lives and didn't finish our education, which makes it hard to get a good job. Or we may have even made our living in the drug trade, so giving up drugs means giving up our source of income too. Perhaps we were or still are in jail or prison because of crimes related to our addiction, and we worry what kind of job we can get if we have a record. Others of us may have a co-occurring mental illness that has kept us out of the job market.

Going back to work or finding a new job after getting sober or going through treatment for an addiction disorder can be challenging and even a little scary. If we had a job when we were using, our work probably suffered. We may have been late to work many times or not shown up at all, which likely made our coworkers or bosses concerned, confused, angry, or resentful. We may have even put other people's jobs in danger by asking them to cover up for us in the past. Some of us were lucky enough to work for people who understand that addiction is a disease. Maybe they gave us time and helped us get into treatment.

If we took time off work to go to treatment, we might feel awkward or embarrassed about going back to our office or company—even when the company has drug policies and programs to help employees with addiction disorders. We might worry that our coworkers will be angry at us because they had to do more work when we were gone. Many of us in a Twelve Step program go back through Steps Four through Nine when we return to work. And when we're ready, we make amends to our bosses, coworkers, clients, or customers if we've harmed them. We apologize for the hurt we may have caused and make a commitment to take responsibility for our actions in the future. If we owe money, we work out a way to pay it back.

Timing is important here; we probably will want to get our feet on the ground and give people a chance to get used to us being back and being sober. Our sponsor, counselor, or clergy person can help us know when the timing is right. We need to also set clear boundaries about how much we disclose and to whom.

Some of us worry that coworkers might treat us with pity

or distrust when we return to our jobs. Or we think they will make things tough for us because they drink or use drugs. This is what happened to Zach when he returned to his construction job.

> Some of the guys on my old crew—and some of the women too—put me down when I got back to work after taking a month off for drug rehab. They gave me a hard time about doing drugs and not being able to hold my liquor, and they sure weren't interested in hearing about recovery. If we ate lunch at places where they could order beer, or if we'd stop for a bite to eat after work, they'd accuse me of spying on them and counting their drinks. It got so I'd just pack a lunch and eat alone in the truck. It got pretty bad and I started to feel kind of lonely—which is a big trigger for me. Our company is pretty big and they have a good Employee Assistance Program (EAP) that helped me get into treatment in the first place, so I decided to talk to them. The woman I saw knew of a foreman who was open about being in recovery, and she thought that crew might be a better fit. So I transferred to that crew. Now I even like going to work. Turns out a couple of other people go to Twelve Step meetings too, so I've made some good friends to hang out with outside of work. And

my girlfriend likes them too, which is huge because
she didn't like most of my old gang. Things are defi-
nitely looking up on the work scene.

Being anxious about going back to work is normal. Stress,
self-consciousness, and even old feelings of shame are common, and we can use our support system to work through
these issues. Chances are our coworkers will be supportive of
our recovery and time away. Most probably have a friend or
family member who has struggled or who is still struggling
with alcohol or other drug problems. It's up to us to decide
how much we want to tell them about our addiction disorder or recovery. Sometimes we might need to socialize at
business lunches or gatherings, and we may feel pressured
to have a drink—or snort or hit. If we aren't comfortable saying we're in recovery, we can say, "No thanks, I don't drink,"
or "I've stopped drinking and using drugs because it was affecting my health." Some of the people we come in contact
with at work might even have problems themselves. They
might ask us for advice or help, which allows us to practice
Step Twelve.

We've learned that recovery isn't about getting rid of all
the stress we have in our lives. Rather, it's about learning how
to cope with difficulties when they do arise. If we have a relapse prevention plan, we can be ready for the tricky situations

that could come up. For example, we might have to go out of town on business—and be away from our support system. This is just what happened to Bill W. when he went on that business trip to Akron we talked about in the first chapter. But we know what to do: Like Bill did when he ended up talking to Dr. Bob for hours, we call our sponsor; find the nearest AA, NA, or other recovery group; and go and talk to other alcoholics or addicts who can help keep us from slipping. If we're not in a Twelve Step group, we call someone in our support network—a family member, friend, or religious or therapy support group member—and talk about the situation and go over our relapse prevention plan. Some of us put off building a support network and creating a relapse prevention plan. If so, we find that getting into a stressful situation like job hunting or traveling is a good time to do it.

Whatever we may experience when we return to work, as Zach realized, we have to make recovery a priority. Zach knew that his work situation could trigger a relapse, and he took action by using the EAP services his company offered. If we are having problems with returning to work and don't have such services available to us, we can still get support from our recovery group, our sponsor, our counselor, our spiritual advisor, or from a friend who understands and supports our recovery. We can also take care of ourselves and our recovery by

- going to recovery or other support meetings regularly
- building and maintaining a strong support network of family, friends, and others who can boost our confidence and listen to our challenges and successes about work
- strictly following any treatment aftercare plan that we created, if we were in treatment
- avoiding job-related drinking events, like happy hour, especially in early recovery
- maintaining a strong relapse prevention plan with lists of our triggers and our common warning signs of relapse, such as changes in mood, sleeping and eating habits, or having thoughts of using

We also work each day to stay in or maintain our recovery, as suggested in Steps Ten and Eleven. We do this by checking in on our emotional state (are we feeling resentful? are there amends we have to make?), our physical state (are we sleeping, eating, and exercising enough to stay healthy?), and our spiritual state (are we doing some form of prayer or meditation daily and staying connected with our higher power?).

Keeping our work lives in balance means not diving into work too quickly when we return to it. We need to avoid working too many hours or becoming obsessed or overly focused on work and bringing it home with us. Certain professions in areas like business, sales, the law, and entertainment have high rates of alcohol and drug use. This may be because these people can financially afford to drink and use, and so it may be a part of their lifestyle. Some people are often able to hide the seriousness of their use because it's accepted and even encouraged in their line of work. Malika, a general practitioner at a very busy inner-city clinic who is recovering from an addiction to Valium and other tranquilizers, discovered how important it was to keep her professional, her spiritual, and her personal life in balance.

> Only my supervisor and one friend from work knew that my leave of absence was because of treatment for drug addiction, and they've been a great source of support. But it's still been hard to keep things in balance now that I'm back at work. Like many docs, I'm a "workaholic" by nature, and I felt this pressure to prove myself because I had been gone for a while. I went a little crazy at first, working sixteen-hour days, offering to sub for other doctors on my days off, and doing other things around the clinic I didn't have to do. Not surprisingly, my daily meditations and check-ins with my sponsor went by the wayside. I was exhausted. Before long, I found myself

actually dreaming about ways to get into the drug cabinet at the clinic. Luckily, I have to be constantly monitored by our state's Health Professionals Services Program (HPSP) or I could lose my medical license. HPSP is a confidential program I have to report to. They keep track of my recovery, my work, and medications I have to take, along with monitoring my attendance at support groups. And they do random urine screens, which is a good thing. Recovering health professionals can't screw up with HPSP watching; if they do, they can get in big trouble. Plus, my supervisor and work friend are wonderful. My friend brought me up short when she said, "Hey Malika, didn't you lose a husband because of your workaholism and drug addiction? You don't want to lose your job too." And my group—a regular old NA group where I'm just another addict—grounds me and reminds me of how critical it is to keep all three legs of the stool—body, mind, and spirit—in balance.

Looking for a new job is stressful. It's especially important during such high-pressure times to go to our Twelve Step or other recovery or support meetings. Here we can get the help and encouragement of others who are going through or who have gone through the same job hassles we're having. If we have dropped out of school, we might decide to get our GED or go back to college or trade school. In this case, we're relieved to find out the schools have guidance counselors who can help us find jobs. Or we might get help in our job search by using services offered through our county, community, or church. Some of us with co-occurring disorders have found that our treatment facility or medical clinic has Supported Employment services, where a Supported Employment Specialist (SE) can help us write a résumé and get references. They can also help us search for work, prepare us for a job interview, help figure out transportation to and from work, help us with job training, and give us suggestions about adjusting to new responsibilities and schedules. An SE can also help us understand things like wages, taxes like Social Security, and benefits like health care. Some of us need other services—including housing, medical, financial, and legal assistance—that are often available either by referral through an SE, social worker, or through our county or state social service agencies. If we're homeless, we usually need to have an address before we can look for a job, so finding housing will be our first priority.

Finding a job is probably even more challenging if we've been recently released or are about to be released from jail or prison or if we have an older criminal record. It might take even more time to get a job we like because we first must prove ourselves to be trustworthy. When we interview for a job, we might think people are looking at us or judging us differently because we're ex-offenders. If that happens, it's important to remember that we can't control the actions or thoughts or beliefs of others—we only have control over our own thoughts and actions. Besides, being turned down may have nothing to do with our criminal history; most people get turned down for jobs. For those of us with records, any job we accept should support our two most important goals: staying sober and staying free of crime. If coworkers or a work environment can draw us into our old addictive thinking patterns, bad things are bound to happen. A counselor from our state's Department of Corrections might be able to provide many of the Supported Employment services described earlier, which could help greatly with our job search. Those of us on parole have often found our parole officers helpful in connecting us with social services that offer financial and career counseling. If we're in a recovery or other support group, we can also see if someone there might know someone who would be able to help us prepare a résumé or brainstorm on how we might find a job. The more people we talk to when looking for work—the larger our network—the more likely we'll be to find a job.

How much we want or need to say about our addiction disorder, mental disorder, or criminal record on a job application, in our résumé, or during an interview depends on the situation and on the law. We want to be straightforward, responsible, simple, and honest—but we want to be smart, too, and know our rights. For example, in U.S. companies with fifteen or more employees, it's against federal law to ask us questions on an application or in an interview about our drug or alcohol disorders because recovered alcoholics or drug addicts are considered to have a disability and are protected under the Americans with Disability Act (ADA). According to ADA rules, an employer can only ask questions about disabilities or require a medical exam after an actual job offer has been made. Some questions about alcohol and drugs are allowed if they aren't asked in a way that would reveal an addiction disorder (a disability). It's always a good idea to check in with someone like our vocational counselor so we know ahead of time what or how much we need, should, or want to tell a potential employer about our alcohol or drug history.

There are also guidelines and laws for what an employer can and cannot ask about our arrest records, criminal records, convictions for the use or sale of illegal drugs, or offenses like driving under the influence of alcohol. So we should check on those laws in our state and community too. In general, a potential employer might be able to ask about our criminal records because things like dealing drugs are not disabilities. However, they can't ask about our arrest records. In some cases, a good answer on an application about our criminal record might be "I do have a criminal record, and I am prepared to discuss it in the interview."

If there are gaps in our employment record due to our using, mental illness, or jail time, we can use our best judgment or get trusted advice about how honest we should or need to be about our past, including our drinking and drug use. We can stress that we're abstinent and that we've changed our lives. Otherwise, if a potential employer might hold our addiction against us, we don't lie, but we can say something general about having gone through some personal changes and how we're now ready to enter the job market. If we've served time for criminal behavior, we don't have to reveal what our crime was or our addiction unless we think the employer will understand. If we do choose to talk about it, we present it in a positive light of being changed. We have found that the best approach is to be positive about ourselves, our abilities, and about the position we're applying for. Showing eagerness to work and willingness to do what it takes to be successful at a particular job counts for a lot.

A growing number of us are retired or approaching retirement age. We have the special challenge of finding meaningful activities and avoiding isolation as we have more time on our hands. We can do this by going to more meetings, sponsoring newcomers, developing hobbies (especially those that involve other people), and volunteering for organizations that do work we believe in. Many of us may also have to make a decision about whether we will use the highly addictive opioid painkillers that are often prescribed for the aches and pains that come with the physical challenges of aging. We have found it helps to be honest with our doctors about our addiction disorder and explore alternatives, such as acupuncture, mindfulness meditation, physical therapy, and nonaddictive painkillers. We need to avoid using opioids and other addictive medications—especially if these were our drugs of choice during active addiction—except in the most extreme circumstances when nothing else helps, and even then under close supervision by a health care professional.

. . .

Work, education, and volunteering can be an important part of our recovery lifestyle. These activities can focus our energy and attention on being productive and positive, which reduces the risk of relapse. A career plan can give us a sense of purpose and the opportunity to choose work that will be yet another way to be of service to others. Our jobs, getting additional education, and volunteer activities can also help us meet more people who might become friends, which can broaden our support network. The downside, however, is that any of these endeavors can also bring stress and pressure that might increase our risk of relapse, so it's important to use our recovery tools to keep ourselves physically, emotionally, and spiritually in balance in whatever kind of work we do.

We're learning how working a program of recovery can make us better sons, daughters, partners, parents, friends, and all-around human beings. When we live lives of recovery at our workplaces, we also become great employees, better supervisors, and more effective in our professions—the kind of workers any employer would be lucky to have.

11

A Community of Recovery

As our cravings and our obsession to find and use alcohol and drugs lessen, we usually discover that our interest for other things grows. We become more ready to move beyond focusing on ourselves and getting high, and we connect with the world again. Now we have a new energy and determination to repair our relationships. We can name and control our feelings and emotions better. We're learning what it means to be intimate and honest with those we love. We're redefining our roles in our family of origin and our current family. And we're finding a healthy sense of place and worth in our work or school. We have these experiences and make these changes at different times and on different schedules, according to the seriousness of our addiction and our life situation.

Many of us have already discovered a community of mutual support—those who help us and those we help stay sober as we travel the path of recovery together. Many of us started our recovery journeys in Twelve Step or other peer recovery groups. And in these groups we continue to find the support we need to stay drug free and emotionally healthy over the long term. When we connect with other people who share their stories of drinking and using, their experiences in recovery, and their messages of strength and hope, we move farther away from a "culture of addiction" toward a new "culture of recovery." We commit to a way of life where addiction no longer controls our thoughts and behaviors. And if we relapse, we have a safe place to connect with others who understand. They can help get us on track again and remind us that relapse doesn't mean we're weak or hopeless— it doesn't mean we have to throw our recovery progress out the window and start over again.

We enter recovery by making a commitment to ourselves, to some power greater than ourselves, to loved ones, and to our recovery community to try to stay sober. But an addiction disorder is a disease that needs to be taken care of or it can return with full force. We take care of it, and ourselves, by practicing a program of recovery for the rest of our lives. We each bring our own needs, backgrounds, and beliefs to whatever program of recovery we choose to practice. At the heart of the program we've talked about in this book are the Twelve Steps, which offer principles and practices of healthy living and guidelines for becoming drug free that have worked for millions of people.

Many of us find that a recovery program provides an "orderliness" to our lives that was often lacking when we were drinking or taking drugs. We learn that by doing certain recovery-related things each day, little by little, we get used to our new sober, healthier, and more fulfilling lifestyle. Some of us, for example, take time each day to pray, meditate, or read something about recovery. Others of us try to connect with someone in recovery each day. In addition to these daily activities, most of us try to get to at least one recovery meeting every week (more in early recovery or a crisis, e.g. relapse) and to do whatever service work we can. Studies have shown that the more Twelve Step meetings we go to and the longer we stay in a program, the less likely we are to relapse.

. . .

We've noted how a number of Twelve Step groups have sprung up around the world since AA was founded in the 1930s and NA in the 1950s. Besides Al-Anon, Alateen, and Nar-Anon for family members of alcoholics and addicts, there are Twelve Step groups that focus on particular drugs, such as Marijuana Anonymous, Pills Anonymous, and Cocaine Anonymous, which is open to all people who desire to be clean and sober regardless of their drug of choice. In addition, there are the three support groups for people with co-occurring addiction and mental health disorders that we've already mentioned:

Double Trouble in Recovery, Dual Diagnosis Anonymous, and Dual Recovery Anonymous. There are also Twelve Step groups for people who are addicted to gambling, sex, overeating, and other compulsive behaviors. Even with all these choices, a group based on the Twelve Steps doesn't work for all of us. Some of us have found help in recovery groups that offer alternatives to the Twelve Steps, such as SMART Recovery, Women for Sobriety, and Secular Organizations for Sobriety. (See appendix C, Recovery Resources, for a more complete list of alternative recovery groups.) Some of us are professionals who have found help with support groups for people in our occupation, including Physicians Serving Physicians, Peer Assistance Program for Nurses, Accountants Concerned for Accountants, Lawyers Concerned for Lawyers, Dentists Concerned for Dentists, and Pharmacists Aiding Pharmacists. Or we might have found the ongoing support we need in groups at our church, synagogue, or temple; in our mental health peer support or therapy group; or in a support group based on a nonreligious spiritual path.

Whatever path to recovery we choose to walk, what most of us have in common is our commitment to

- working a daily program of recovery that includes a relapse prevention plan

- staying connected in a meaningful way with a power

greater than ourselves through daily meditation and supportive relationships with other people

- finding a way to be of service to others, including the alcoholic and addict who still suffers

Those of us in Twelve Step peer recovery groups believe that those groups are successful in large part because they are truly run by us—the members—without any outside individual or organization setting the rules or trying to influence how our groups operate. Our members share a single purpose: to deal with a particular addiction. The only requirement for AA membership is the *desire* to stop drinking; for NA, the only requirement is the *desire* to stop using drugs. This is true for other recovery groups as well.

AA and the other groups that grew out of it follow the Twelve Traditions that were written by AA's cofounder, Bill W. These Traditions lay out the principles and values that guide group behavior. They also list ways that members can make sure their groups are of the people and for the people they are intended to help. (See appendix A for a list of the Twelve Traditions). At the heart of the Traditions is anonymity—an understanding that the identities of members who attend a Twelve Step group will be protected. Anonymity was especially important in the early days of AA, when the stigma of alcoholism was greater and before it was officially recognized as an addiction disorder. Anonymity is still important because an agreement to honor privacy and confidences ("What is said in the room stays in the room") builds trust in our groups. When we go to a meeting, we know that we can say anything and not be afraid of having that trust betrayed. Anonymity is also a great "equalizer"— which means that inside the walls of a meeting space, no one is different or better than any other member.

While Twelve Step members do not reveal anything about *another* member of the group, any one of us may choose to go public with our own story. That is, we are free to let the world beyond our group know that we're in recovery. Some of us are involved in movements like Faces and Voices of Recovery that actually encourage recovering people to go public as a way to lessen the stigma of addiction. Sharing our identity as addicts and telling our success stories can counter the negative stories that we too often see in the media. If we don't talk about belonging to a particular group but say something like, "I'm John Smith, and I've been in long-term recovery now for twenty-four years," we are not breaking the Traditions.

We have a choice of several different kinds of Twelve Step meetings we can attend—there's no "one size fits all." For example, our meetings are either "open" or "closed." In an open meeting, people don't have to be an alcoholic or drug addict to attend. They might be there to learn more about addiction or because they think they might have a problem but aren't ready to commit to a program of recovery. Closed meetings are for those of us who already know we have a problem and have a sincere desire to stop drinking or using. In this case, for example, alcoholics would go to an AA closed meeting; other drug users would go to a closed meeting of NA or another group that focuses on their drug of choice.

Most Twelve Step meetings generally follow the AA meeting format:

- At speaker meetings, a volunteer from the group or a guest from another group tells his or her personal story or speaks about one of the Steps or a theme from the Big Book or NA basic text. In some speaker meetings, members have a chance to share their thoughts about how the speaker's story relates to their own recovery path.

- Big Book meetings focus on certain readings and have group discussions where members talk about a topic or section from the Big Book.

- At Step meetings, a member volunteers to give a short talk about a Step (or sometimes one of the Traditions), which is then discussed by the group. Each member has a chance to relate his or her own situation and story to that Step.

- At topic meetings, a group member might want to discuss something that is important to group members, such as sponsorship or emotional sobriety. If other members agree, the member who requested the discussion leads the talk, and members may choose to share their thoughts on how the topic relates to their own experience.

In addition to the kinds of meetings listed above, if we live in larger cities we can usually find Twelve Step meetings that attract people from our particular culture, race, gender, sexual orientation, or language. For example, there are African American, Asian American, Latino, and Native American groups; groups for men only or women only; GLBT (gay, lesbian, bisexual, and transgender) groups; and groups for recent Hispanic, Asian, or African immigrants. And, as we've already mentioned, there are groups that focus on a particular drug, such as Cocaine Anonymous (CA), or that are designed for addicts who also have a mental disorder. CA has attracted a lot of young people as well as people addicted to other drugs besides cocaine. You can also find AA and NA groups for teens and young adults, as well as groups that attract older people. Beatrice, now ninety, found that she was most comfortable in a group of people closer to her age. Here's her story.

I rarely touched alcohol when I was young because I was taught that "proper ladies don't drink." After I was married, I'd sometimes have a drink when we'd go out with friends or when we entertained. But my husband died when I was seventy-two, and I was so depressed and lonely that I started drinking wine—then vodka—every night, just to numb the pain a little. My drinking got worse and worse, but I only drank in private because I was also brought up to believe that alcoholism was something only bums on skid row had. My daughter worried that I had the start of dementia, and she finally got me to go see my doctor, who prescribed antidepressants. I didn't tell him about the drinking—but things got worse, especially when I started taking the pills he prescribed and didn't stop drinking. Then my daughter stopped by my apartment one night unexpectedly and found me passed out next to an empty vodka bottle. So, as we used to say, "the jig was up," and this time she went to the doctor with me. He arranged for me to get an assessment for addiction, where I learned about late-onset alcoholism and how it can come on faster in elderly people. I went through treatment, but everyone in the group was so much younger. They were all very nice, but it was like they were talking a different language. I had no idea about what they were saying when they talked about their partying or drugs, or about "tweeting" or texting or such things. And I'm sure they couldn't relate to me or to many of my issues. Luckily, shortly after I got out of treatment, I moved into an assisted living place and they have AA meetings right in my building. It was such a relief to find a group of people closer to my age who have a lot of the same experiences and problems. We can laugh about our aches and pains, and even cry together about missing people we've lost. And, most important, we can talk about our addiction without feeling odd or ashamed.

Like people, every Twelve Step meeting and group has its own personality. This means that, when we can, we try to find one where we feel comfortable and welcome. If someone hasn't already suggested a meeting to us, we check online to see which recovery groups might have meetings near us. Many of us try out a few meetings before we find one that fits our needs and personality. We can learn and get support from all kinds of people, so we don't need to find a group whose members are "just like us." What's most important is that we find good models in recovery. We do our best to find a meeting we'll look forward to attending every week. We look for a meeting where we feel safe and that gives us a foundation on which we can build a solid recovery with others who share our desire to live sane and sober. We go to as many groups and as often as we need to. In the beginning of our recovery, the recommendation to do "ninety meetings in ninety days" is a good one. If we're unemployed or retired, we might even want to attend one or more meetings a day because it's a safe place to be and we don't have to be by ourselves. If we have a bad or uncomfortable experience with one or two groups, we simply try a different one. Here's what Emmett, a forty-three-year-old African American man, experienced.

> When I got out of prison after doing five years for dealing cocaine, I was scared about how I was going to stay away from the people I'd been running with. I didn't know how I was going to find people to hang with who didn't do drugs. I was pretty lucky in two ways: People from NA would come to my facility and hold meetings, so I got a pretty good start on the Twelve Steps and had even done my Fifth Step with one of the guys who ran the meetings. Plus, my parole officer understood recovery and he got me online to find NA and AA in town because I did both alcohol and cocaine. He said I should do ninety meetings in ninety days to get my feet on the ground. The first NA meeting I went to was great. There were a lot of different people from different backgrounds. There

was even a woman who had done some time, so we had some things to talk about after the meeting. Now, my second meeting was a different story. It was an all-male AA meeting, which I thought would be good for me. But when I got there, there were a bunch of rich white dudes sitting around talking about their group golf tournament and how much money they'd lost in the stock market when they were using. I think somebody said hello when I walked in, but otherwise nobody said boo to me. When my turn to talk came around, I just passed. After the meeting, these guys started talking to each other again and pretty much ignored me, so I split. When I was waiting for my bus, I started thinking about going back to my old neighborhood to see who was still around. But then I remembered what my parole officer had told me about trying different meetings, so I just pulled out my meeting list, crossed this one off it, and looked to see what meeting was happening the next day. I'm really grateful that I had that good experience my first meeting because if that male group had been my first meeting, I don't know if I would have kept going. As it is, I'm clean six months now, and that first meeting I went to has become my home group.

The best meetings are those where we can be honest about our addiction and not be judged. In most established Twelve Step meetings, we can feel confident that what we say in a meeting will stay there—that our confidentiality and anonymity will be respected because of the Twelve Traditions. When we go to a meeting, we try not to take part in any "cross-talk," where members pick apart what people say or give advice. We try to remember that we're only responsible for taking our own inventory—not anyone else's. We also avoid what is called "thirteenth stepping"—flirting or making sexual advances toward another member. We try to remember that a romantic relationship with another group member can mess up our recovery, especially in the first year. We don't treat meetings as a dating service.

Our meetings usually take place in pretty simple settings where the rent is cheap, which is why they're often in churches. The Steps and Traditions are sometimes posted on the wall, along with popular slogans that help us remember key ideas in working our program. We've talked about some of these already, like "Easy does it," "A day at a time," "Bring the body and the mind will follow," and "Let go and let God." There are also acronyms like HALT (hungry, angry, lonely, and tired), and HOW (honesty, openness, and willingness). Here are some other helpful slogans and reminders we often use: "It works if you work it," "You have to give it away to keep it," and "KISS" (keep it simple stupid).

While all our meetings are different, most follow a similar pattern. After everyone takes a seat, someone who has volunteered to lead the meeting calls the meeting to order. Then he or she reads a short passage from the group's basic text (such as the AA Big Book or NA text) that welcomes everyone and briefly outlines the basic principles for attending the group. Then people take turns introducing themselves by saying something like, "Hi, I'm John, and I'm an alcoholic" (for AA) or, "I'm Mary, I'm an addict" (for NA), or maybe, "Hi, I'm Lee, and I'm an alcoholic and an addict." At some point, a hat or basket is usually passed around to collect small donations. If we can afford it, this helps cover the cost of renting the space and paying for refreshments and any special activities the group may plan. Most meetings will include a welcome to newcomers and a celebration of any recovery anniversaries—where members with a certain amount of time sober receive medallions (also called "chips"). Then, there's usually sharing by each member on the topic or Step covered in that meeting, with everyone having the option to pass. Meetings often close with the Serenity Prayer, although some more traditional meetings close with the Lord's Prayer. We are free to participate in meetings at whatever level is most comfortable for us.

It's usually in our meetings that we find a sponsor. As we've mentioned in other chapters, our sponsor is someone with at least a couple of years of sobriety, who is well grounded in recovery and has experience with the Twelve Steps. This should be someone we can trust to keep our confidences and who can help us work the Steps. We don't expect a sponsor to be our therapist, best friend, lover, or someone who will give us loans or advice on anything that isn't related to our recovery. If we think someone might make a good sponsor—as long as they are of the same sex if we are straight and the opposite sex if we are gay or lesbian—we simply ask if they are willing. If someone doesn't accept, we just ask someone else. Many sponsors limit the number of people they sponsor, or they may have other good reasons why they are unable to sponsor us.

. . .

We are grateful to the AA and NA pioneers who have given us a blueprint for action and a foundation for change—a way to climb out of the darkness and hopelessness of addiction and toward the hope and promise of a new way to live. We have shared what we have learned from their teachings in this book and invited you to try what's worked for us. Although our lives, experiences, and paths to recovery are very different, we still have a common bond—we have an addiction disorder and a desire to live a life free from mind-altering drugs.

The suggestions we share in this book come from our own stories and from what we've learned from addiction professionals about what works in treating this disorder of the body, mind, and spirit.

We know from experience that the path of recovery isn't always easy. There are times when we will stumble and fall back, but we have found a way to get ourselves back on track. We remember that recovery is about progress, not perfection. We are equal and flawed beings doing the best we can as we walk this path together, living a life of possibility with a renewed sense of hope and purpose—one day at a time. We hope, as did Bill W. in the closing chapter 11 of the Big Book, that "you will surely meet some of us as you trudge the Road of Happy Destiny."[1]

---

1. *Alcoholics Anonymous,* 4th ed. (New York: Alcoholics Anonymous World Services, 2001), 164.

APPENDIX A

The Twelve Steps of Alcoholics Anonymous

Page 196

The Twelve Steps of Narcotics Anonymous

Page 197

The Twelve Traditions of Alcoholics Anonymous

Page 198

The Twelve Steps of Alcoholics Anonymous

1. We admitted we were powerless over alcohol—that our lives had become unmanageable.

2. Came to believe that a power greater than ourselves could restore us to sanity.

3. Made a decision to turn our will and our lives over to the care of God *as we understood Him.*

4. Made a searching and fearless moral inventory of ourselves.

5. Admitted to God, to ourselves, and to another human being the exact nature of our wrongs.

6. Were entirely ready to have God remove all these defects of character.

7. Humbly asked Him to remove our shortcomings.

8. Made a list of all persons we had harmed, and became willing to make amends to them all.

9. Made direct amends to such people wherever possible, except when to do so would injure them or others.

10. Continued to take personal inventory and when we were wrong promptly admitted it.

11. Sought through prayer and meditation to improve our conscious contact with God *as we understood Him,* praying only for knowledge of His will for us and the power to carry that out.

12. Having had a spiritual awakening as the result of these steps, we tried to carry this message to alcoholics, and to practice these principles in all our affairs.

Alcoholics Anonymous, 4th ed. (New York: Alcoholics Anonymous World Services, 2001), 59–60. The Twelve Steps are reprinted with permission of Alcoholics Anonymous World Services, Inc. ("AAWS"). Permission to reprint the Twelve Steps does not mean that AAWS has reviewed or approved the contents of this publication, or that A.A. necessarily agrees with the views expressed herein. A.A. is a program of recovery from alcoholism only—use of the Twelve Steps in connection with programs and activities which are patterned after A.A., but which address other problems, or in any other non-A.A. context, does not imply otherwise.

The Twelve Steps of Narcotics Anonymous

1. We admitted that we were powerless over our addiction, that our lives had become unmanageable.

2. We came to believe that a Power greater than ourselves could restore us to sanity.

3. We made a decision to turn our will and our lives over to the care of God *as we understood Him.*

4. We made a searching and fearless moral inventory of ourselves.

5. We admitted to God, to ourselves, and to another human being the exact nature of our wrongs.

6. We were entirely ready to have God remove all these defects of character.

7. We humbly asked Him to remove our shortcomings.

8. We made a list of all persons we had harmed, and became willing to make amends to them all.

9. We made direct amends to such people wherever possible, except when to do so would injure them or others.

10. We continued to take personal inventory and when we were wrong promptly admitted it.

11. We sought through prayer and meditation to improve our conscious contact with God *as we understood Him,* praying only for knowledge of His will for us and the power to carry that out.

12. Having had a spiritual awakening as a result of these steps, we tried to carry this message to addicts, and to practice these principles in all our affairs.

The Twelve Traditions of Alcoholics Anonymous

1. Our common welfare should come first; personal recovery depends upon A.A. unity.

2. For our group purpose there is but one ultimate authority—a loving God as He may express Himself in our group conscience. Our leaders are but trusted servants; they do not govern.

3. The only requirement for A.A. membership is a desire to stop drinking.

4. Each group should be autonomous except in matters affecting other groups or A.A. as a whole.

5. Each group has but one primary purpose—to carry its message to the alcoholic who still suffers.

6. An A.A. group ought never endorse, finance, or lend the A.A. name to any related facility or outside enterprise, lest problems of money, property, and prestige divert us from our primary purpose.

7. Every A.A. group ought to be fully self-supporting, declining outside contributions.

8. Alcoholics Anonymous should remain forever nonprofessional, but our service centers may employ special workers.

9. A.A., as such, ought never be organized; but we may create service boards or committees directly responsible to those they serve.

10. Alcoholics Anonymous has no opinion on outside issues; hence the A.A. name ought never be drawn into public controversy.

11. Our public relations policy is based on attraction rather than promotion; we need always maintain personal anonymity at the level of press, radio, and films.

12. Anonymity is the spiritual foundation of all our traditions, ever reminding us to place principles before personalities.

Twelve Steps and Twelve Traditions (New York: Alcoholics Anonymous World Services, 1981). The Twelve Traditions are reprinted with permission of Alcoholics Anonymous World Services, Inc. ("AAWS"). Permission to reprint the Twelve Traditions does not mean that AAWS has reviewed or approved the contents of this publication, or that A.A. necessarily agrees with the views expressed herein. A.A. is a program of recovery from alcoholism <u>only</u>—use of the Twelve Traditions in connection with programs and activities which are patterned after A.A., but which address other problems, or in any other non-A.A. context, does not imply otherwise.

Common Drugs of Abuse

Drugs of abuse are substances that people use to change how they feel, which is why they are also called mood-altering chemicals. These might be illegal drugs like meth, cocaine, or heroin; or they may be legal for adults only, like alcohol and tobacco. Medicines that treat illness can also become drugs of abuse when people take them to get high—not because they're sick and following their doctor's orders. People can even abuse cough or cold medicines from the store if they ignore directions and take too much at one time.

Alcohol (drinks like beer, malt liquor, wine, and "hard liquor" like whiskey, rum, or gin)

- **Some signs of use/abuse:** Alcohol smell on breath or clothes, drunken behavior (loud talk and laughter; slurred speech; throwing up; violence; poor coordination; hangover; passing or blacking out)

- **Possible dangers/side effects:** Fatal alcohol poisoning; strokes, cancer, liver disease, and other diseases; brain damage from long-term use; unsafe sex, which can lead to HIV/AIDS and hepatitis (a liver disease). People are also more likely to get hurt or killed when they're drunk or cause harm to others; babies of alcoholics can be born with mental retardation and other health problems; addiction

Tobacco (cigarettes, cigars, chewing tobacco, or other products that contain the drug nicotine)

- **Some signs of use/abuse:** Cigarette smell on breath, clothes, or hair; smokers' cough; shortness of breath; frequent spitting (if a person chews)

- **Possible dangers/side effects:** Lung cancer and emphysema for smokers and those who breathe their smoke; heart disease; tooth loss and mouth cancer for those who chew tobacco; tobacco addiction can affect unborn children and children who breathe cigarette smoke; addiction

Cannabis/marijuana (weed, pot)/hashish (hash): psychoactive ingredient THC (Tetrahydrocannabinol)

- **Some signs of use/abuse:** Very thirsty or hungry (have "munchies"); bloodshot eyes; trouble with thinking, memory, and learning; silliness and laughter for no reason; sleepiness; dizziness; being anxious or talkative

- **Possible dangers/effects:** Same coughing and breathing problems as smoking cigarettes; memory and heart problems; trouble concentrating; loss of interest and caring; drugged driving; addiction

Synthetic marijuana (like K2 and spice)

- **Some signs of use/abuse:** Hallucinations; anxiety and confusion; pale appearance; vomiting; extreme paranoia

- **Possible dangers/side effects:** High blood pressure; heart attacks; hallucinations and other uncomfortable side effects; addiction

Stimulants (Speed)

Cocaine (coke, crack)

- **Some signs of use/abuse:** Mood swings; being talkative or restless; confusion; heightened sexuality; paranoia; nosebleeds if snorted; needle marks if injected; weight loss

- **Possible dangers/side effects:** Heart attack and stroke; HIV/AIDS and hepatitis from shooting up or having unsafe sex; addiction

Methamphetamine (meth, crank, ice)

- **Some signs of use/abuse:** Mood swings; too much energy and talkativeness; burns on lips or fingers from hot meth pipe; skin sores from scratching; stained, broken, and rotten teeth; weight loss; users can look old and ill

- **Possible dangers/side effects:** Hot body temperature can cause users to pass out and die; HIV/AIDS and hepatitis from shooting up or having unsafe sex; addiction

Methylphenidates and amphetamines (like Ritalin)

- **Some signs of use/abuse:** Feelings of hostility and paranoia; trouble sleeping and eating, which can lead to malnutrition

- **Possible dangers/side effects:** Increased blood pressure, heart rate, and body temperature, which can lead to serious heart attacks and strokes; addiction

Synthetics like "bath salts"

- **Some signs of use/abuse:** Similar to cocaine, meth, and other amphetamine use; panic attacks

- **Possible dangers/side effects:** Hallucinations; increased heart rate and blood pressure; dehydration and kidney failure; breakdown of skeletal muscle tissue; ten times more dopamine released in brain than cocaine; addiction

Opiates/opioids (like morphine, opium, heroin, and prescription painkillers)

Heroin

- **Some signs of use/abuse:** Very small pupils; slow thinking and movements; sleepiness and dreaminess; needle marks on skin if users shoot up; vomiting; itchy skin

- **Possible dangers/side effects:** Slowed down or stopped breathing and death; HIV/AIDS and hepatitis from shooting up and sharing needles; overdose and death because users can't tell how strong drug is until they take it (signs of overdose are slow breathing, blue lips and fingernails, cold and clammy skin, and shaking); coma; addiction

Prescription painkillers (like oxycodone, OxyContin, or Percocet)

- **Some signs of abuse:** Very small pupils; vomiting; "doctor shopping" (secretly visiting many different doctors to get as many prescriptions as possible); diarrhea; nervousness or anger or sad feelings; muscle and bone pain and chills

- **Possible dangers/side effects:** Slowed down or stopped breathing and death; coma; overdose and death; addiction

Sedatives (like benzodiazepines, barbiturates, and sleep medications)

- **Some signs of abuse:** Slurred speech; shallow breathing; fatigue; disorientation; poor coordination; feeling excited or high

- **Possible dangers/side effects:** Coma; respiratory distress (breathing slows or stops) and death; addiction

Hallucinogens (like LSD, psilocybin mushrooms, and mescaline)

- **Some signs of use/abuse:** Hallucinations; mood swings; distorted senses (hearing, seeing, and feeling things that aren't there); high sensitivity to colors, smells, lights, and sounds; dilated (big) pupils; silliness and laughter for no reason

- **Possible dangers/side effects:** Fatal accidents because of terrifying thoughts and feelings; higher body temperature, heart rate, and blood pressure; "bad trips" (experiences while high) that can last up to twelve hours

Club drugs (like Ecstasy, GHB, Rohypnol, and ketamine)

Ecstasy

- **Some signs of use/abuse:** Similar to amphetamines and mescaline; increased energy, feeling excited and high; distorted sense of time; sometimes called the "love drug" because it makes users feel overly friendly and "touchy"; blurred vision; paranoia; insomnia

- **Possible dangers/side effects:** High blood pressure and body temperature; high heart rate; convulsions

GHB (gamma hydroxybutyrate)

- **Some signs of use/abuse:** Sleepiness; nausea; dizziness; amnesia

- **Possible dangers/side effects:** Coma and death; seizures; often called a "date rape" drug because someone can secretly put it in another person's drink and have sex with them without their consent because they are passed out; addiction

Rohypnol (also called "Roofies")

- **Some signs of use/abuse:** Slurred speech; confusion; weakness; trouble walking; amnesia

- **Possible dangers/side effects:** Can be lethal when mixed with alcohol; also called a "date rape" drug; addiction

Ketamine (also called K or Special K)

- **Some signs of use/abuse:** Withdrawn behavior; sleepiness;

distraction; makes users feel far away from what's going on around them; scary and unpleasant feelings

- **Possible dangers/side effects:** Impaired motor functions; high blood pressure and potentially fatal respiratory problems; addiction

PCP (phencyclidine; also called angel or angel dust)

- **Some signs of use/abuse:** Many dramatic behavior changes, including anger, violence, or unhappiness; dizziness; unsteadiness; makes users feel far away and dreamy; nausea

- **Possible dangers/side effects:** Suicidal tendencies; at high doses, blood pressure, pulse, and breathing rates drop; hallucinations; addiction

Anabolic Steroids

- **Some signs of use/abuse:** Rapid weight and muscle gain; fast recovery from injuries; aggression; depression and mood swings; changes in appetite; jaundice (yellow skin); purple and red spots on body; swollen feet and legs; trembling; dark skin; bad breath; bad acne; early balding

- **Possible dangers/side effects:** Liver damage; high blood pressure; increased "bad" cholesterol; shrunken testicles; breast development; infertility. Females risk growth of facial hair; menstrual changes; baldness; and deepened voice. Teens risk stunted height; early puberty; severe acne. All users risk infectious diseases such as HIV/AIDS and hepatitis—especially those users who inject the drug—and addiction

Inhalants (dangerous chemicals found in household cleaners, spray cans, glue, and even permanent markers)

- **Some signs of use/abuse:** Sensitivity to light; slurred speech; drowsiness; unconsciousness; runny nose and/or watery eyes; loss of muscle control; sores on nose and mouth; traces of paint or other substances on face and hands; dizziness

- **Possible dangers/side effects:** Passing out; stopped breathing and heart, causing death; hearing loss; spasms; brain damage; bone marrow damage; suffocation; addiction

Recovery Resources

Alcoholics Anonymous World Services, www.aa.org

Narcotics Anonymous World Services, www.na.org

Al-Anon Family Groups, www.Al-anon.alateen.org

Nar-Anon Family Groups, www.nar-anon.org

Cocaine Anonymous, www.ca.org

Crystal Meth Anonymous, www.crystalmeth.org

Heroin Anonymous, www.heroin-anonymous.org

Pills Anonymous, www.pillsanonymous.org

Marijuana Anonymous, www.marijuana-anonymous.org

Co-Dependents Anonymous World Fellowship (CoDA), www.coda.org

Substance Abuse and Mental Health Services Administration (SAMHSA) treatment finder, www.samhsa.gov/treatment

Hazelden Foundation, www.hazelden.org; 24-hour helpline: 800-257-7810

Alcoholics Anonymous, 4th edition. New York: Alcoholics Anonymous World Services, Inc., 2001.

Twelve Steps and Twelve Traditions. New York: Alcoholics Anonymous World Services, Inc., 1981.

Narcotics Anonymous, 6th edition. Van Nuys, CA: Narcotics Anonymous World Services, Inc., 2008.

The Narcotics Anonymous Step Working Guides. Van Nuys, CA: Narcotics Anonymous World Services, Inc., 1998.

Living Sober. New York: Alcoholics Anonymous World Services, 1976.

Getting Started in AA, by Hamilton B. Center City, MN: Hazelden, 1995.

Finding a Home Group, by James G. Center City, MN: Hazelden, 2011.

Undrunk: A Skeptic's Guide to AA, by A. J. Adams. Center City, MN: Hazelden, 2009.

Twenty-Four Hours a Day. Center City, MN: Hazelden, 1975.

Each Day a New Beginning: Daily Meditations for Women, by Karen Casey. Center City, MN: Hazelden, 1982.

A Woman's Way through the Twelve Steps, by Stephanie Covington. Center City, MN: Hazelden, 1994.

Hazelden, a national nonprofit organization founded in 1949, helps people reclaim their lives from the disease of addiction. Built on decades of knowledge and experience, Hazelden offers a comprehensive approach to addiction that addresses the full range of patient, family, and professional needs, including treatment and continuing care for youth and adults, research, higher learning, public education and advocacy, and publishing.

A life of recovery is lived "one day at a time." Hazelden publications, both educational and inspirational, support and strengthen lifelong recovery. In 1954, Hazelden published *Twenty-Four Hours a Day,* the first daily meditation book for recovering alcoholics, and Hazelden continues to publish works to inspire and guide individuals in treatment and recovery, and their loved ones. Professionals who work to prevent and treat addiction also turn to Hazelden for evidence-based curricula, informational materials, and videos for use in schools, treatment programs, and correctional programs.

Through published works, Hazelden extends the reach of hope, encouragement, help, and support to individuals, families, and communities affected by addiction and related issues.

For questions about Hazelden publications,
please call **800-328-9000**
or visit us online at **hazelden.org/bookstore.**